MW00831050

blows to the head

ee
excelsior editions
AN IMPRINT OF STATE UNIVERSITY OF NEW YORK PRESS

blows to the head

how boxing changed my mind

Binnie Klein

Published by
STATE UNIVERSITY OF NEW YORK PRESS, ALBANY

© 2010 State University of New York

All rights reserved

Printed in the United States of America

No part of this book may be used or reproduced in any manner whatsoever without written permission. No part of this book may be stored in a retrieval system or transmitted in any form or by any means including electronic, electrostatic, magnetic tape, mechanical, photocopying, recording, or otherwise without the prior permission in writing of the publisher.

For information, contact
State University of New York Press, Albany, NY
www.sunypress.edu

Production and book design, Laurie Searl
Marketing, Fran Keneston

Library of Congress Cataloging in Publication Data

Klein, Binnie.
Blows to the head : how boxing changed my mind / Binnie Klein. — Excelsior editions.
p. cm.
ISBN 978-1-4384-3001-0 (hardcover : alk. paper)
1. Klein, Binnie. 2. Boxers (Sports)—United States—Biography.
I. Title.
GV1132.K55B69 2010
796.83092–dc22
[B] 2009018960

10 9 8 7 6 5 4 3 2 1

I have no need for the past, I thought, like a child.
I did not consider that the past might have a need for me.

—JONATHAN SAFRAN FOER

contents

prologue

A bloody mouthguard floats in a bucket that I am holding under a young Hispanic man's face. It is a frantic moment between rounds and I am working the corner, reaching through the ropes of the boxing ring and mopping his dark kinky hair with a torn white towel. Inside the ring, kneeling at Manuel's feet and urging him to stay alert, is his coach John, a former middleweight champion. I am a fifty-five-year-old Jewish psychotherapist and spend my days in a leather recliner, quietly tuning myself to the complex themes of other peoples' melodies, and each day begins with someone else's song. But not this night; this night I am edgy, tough, ageless, and loud. A young black disc jockey in the back of the gym cues up the seductive riff of a Spanish dance tune, interweaving it with pounding hip-hop. Three police officers stand near the door, keeping an eye on things.

Manuel complained of nausea before the fight, saying, "I don't know why I feel so weird," and I walked him around the gym, offering my half-eaten jelly doughnut and a firm arm around his shoulder.

It's his first fight. Tending Manuel is so different from my daily work, free of psychological ambiguity and nuance. I'm in the physical dimension. It's the Bizarro World of Superman comics—everything is opposite.

When we first enter the ring, the referee strides over to check Manuel's readiness. "You got your cup?" he asks. Manuel looks stricken, and John and I freeze. The ref frowns, already impatient at our incompetence. A chorus of dissatisfied murmurs rises from the front row and the judging table. Everything is grinding to a halt. Am I in the middle of a dream turning sour, like when you must move but can't move, or scream but no sound comes out? I yell into the crowd where I can see Ryan, our boy who already fought and won, standing next to his proud father who set up a punching bag in their suburban garage when his son was five years old. "Ryan! We need your cup!" Ryan speeds into the locker room like the Pied Piper of penis protection holding up a leather codpiece out of a Brueghel painting, as Manuel leaps over the ropes to follow. They disappear through a door at the back of the gym. A balding and paunchy official straight out of central casting has approached me with a stern expression. "No cup? No fight!" "We're getting it!" I plead. Because this is an amateur event, we're granted leniency. Manuel bursts into the ring, his manhood enhanced by equipment and his own unflagging courage.

The match is saved. It's not a bad dream. I start the encouraging whispers: "Get in there, you can do it, dart in and out like a mosquito, keep busy, jab, jab." I'm not even thinking of Muhammad Ali's famous "sting like a bee"—I fancy I'm inventing an insect image right on the spot. Ideas and words pop up like cartoon balloons, snippets of dialogue from old black-and-white movies where boxers have their egos massaged or are bullied by their managers. Men encouraging men. "Do it for me!" "Live the dream for me!"

"Manuel!" I bellow from the ropes. My throat is sore, and I'm jumping up and down. Thank god for my industrial-strength sports bra. "Get busy! Attaboy!" His graceful body is my avatar. Manuel works at a retail store, and has the gentle manner of a kindly teacher, his face sculpted and handsome. As a successful boxer back in his homeland of Puerto Rico, he would be a warrior who could represent the island. For good or bad, boxing is a sport that celebrates, exploits, and pulls out the pride in ethnicity like a taffy machine.

Manuel starts out too cautious; we're screaming at him to jab. His opponent tries for body blows and we're worried, but suddenly Manuel lets loose a swarm of insistent punches. Three tense rounds later, our fighter is victorious. The crowd cheers, all languages mixed together in a cascade of triumphant pleasure. Mysteriously, Manuel is hard on himself. "I could have fought better. I just didn't have it tonight." "Are you kidding?" I say, "You won!" And it is as simple as that. Winning is everything, well almost everything, in this game. There is also the gorgeous notion of "heart," which is a special kind of courage and persistence. I walk him out of the ring toward Samantha, the ringside physician, who grins at me. The fight promoter, the referee, the physician, the coach . . . they all know me. Sam snaps on her latex gloves for the post-fight physical and checks Manuel's jaw, arms, and eyes. "He's good to go."

I dump the contents of the bucket outside the back door. Working the corner is not the sexiest of jobs. I waited three hours for Manuel's bout, and, just like the excitement, the crash comes quickly, a dip in psychic blood sugar. It's 11 p.m., and it's been a good night, but I'm tired of the flickering fluorescent lights and ready to go home.

The crowd is dispersing; Manuel's was the last bout in tonight's amateur lineup. Baked goods are now discounted to half-price at the concession stand run by the Hamden High School cheerleaders, who have outfitted themselves in bright pink bows and spandex tights. Young mothers scoop up their babies, who have slept or wept through the fights.

Manuel ambles over to the American flag to get his picture taken holding his coveted trophy as the disc jockey cues up Madonna. I hold his infant son and offer his young wife a handkerchief for her tears of pride.

Suddenly the warning tones of my Polish grandmother echo in my ears: "Vos is dos?" (What is this?) I see her standing before me in her plain housedress, legs bowed and encased in thick support stockings, a handkerchief on her head as she lights candles for Shabbas, a woman who traveled on a large ship to the United States in 1921, escaping the impoverished conditions of her shtetl, a woman old before her time and full of fear. Her brows crinkle with confusion, like most people when they hear that I am involved with boxing. Aggression? Physicality? In her shtetl in Poland, often the poorest of dwellings had a special honored shelf for books, and the Jewish way was to observe and study, not to fight. Anything else was a *shanda*, a shame.

"What can I tell you, Grandma? I love it."

1
a dirty sport

"Come on baby, that punch wasn't sexy—put your hips into it."

I am learning how to perfect my jab in an inner-city gym where you can work out for $9.95 a month and then pop next door to the unemployment office to pick up your check. One of a chain of low-cost fitness centers, it is homogenized, no-frills, and this branch is especially low on the chain. The first time I bounded into the gym, hoping to convince John to "take me on," a scrawled sign on an easel warned me that there were to be positively, absolutely no "doo-rags."

Doo-rags?

I was relatively sure I wasn't wearing one.

John "The Punisher" Spehar, my coach, is a 200-pound unusual brute, physically a cross between Bruce Willis and Tony Soprano. His hobby is studying the French Revolution. My Venus of Willendorff belly is flopping as I lurch forward and try to make contact with his leather punch mitts, brown cushions around ten inches wide; up by his shoulder height, they make him look like an angry bear coming out of hibernation.

My hobby is boxing.

I'm mesmerized by my coach, perhaps because he is a happier and more vigorous version of my father. On the road as a traveling salesman, with his Oldsmobile trunk stuffed with sample cases, Julius Alexander Klein (a.k.a. Jay) was funny, warm, clever—beloved by the brokers he visited all over his territory—but at home he left the personable "Salesman of the Year" at the door and in came "Sullen Man," full of fury at being exploited by his cousins who ran Phoenix Candy company, and exuding the malignant depression that fell over my mother, my sisters, and me like a moldy blanket.

Given their strong resemblance to thugs from B movies of the 1940s, I can see John and my father hanging out together. As a teenager, my father drove the family bakery truck in the immigrant neighborhoods of Brooklyn and knew many shady characters. I can imagine him regaling John with his bombastic tale of the day he got a gun from "Ike the Toad" (ah, such names!), and I can hear the theme from *The Sopranos—woke up this morning/got yourself a gu-un*. My father was infatuated with "Alice the Moll" who belonged to Louis "Lepke" Buchalter's gang, Murder, Inc. (The nickname Lepke means "Little Louis" in Yiddish and Murder, Inc. was known as the Jewish Mafia.) Lepke started out pushcart shoplifting, a particularly heartless crime, since pushcart peddlers often had just one pan to sell, one egg, one chicken. He had a henchman, Abe Reles, who did most of the dirty work. Peter Falk played Reles in the movie, *Murder, Inc.* Buchalter was the only major mob boss to have been executed by government authorities for his many murders. In the first season of *The Sopranos* HBO series, Dr. Melfi listens as another psychiatrist talks about his own family's ties through Buchalter to Murder, Inc. The writers had done their homework.

Alice's job for Murder, Inc. was to lure unsuspecting men into parked cars on Pitkin Avenue, where gangsters crouched silently in backseats waiting to beat and rob them. She got unlucky, though, when one of her targets turned out to be a plainclothes cop. When she got out of "stir" she and my father began a tempestuous affair. This was 1932—they were both twenty-one years old, and by then Buchalter controlled a huge assortment of industries and unions in New York, including bakery drivers. My father's family was surely the victim of Buchalter's extortions.

The mob wanted Alice back—she'd been a good earner—and word spreads that they're coming for her. My father has decided to boldly protect Alice, so when the gangsters' ominous black limo arrives, he courageously protests: "She stays where she is!" But it turns out the "Toad" was running late, and when he finally did show up, he shoved a lumpy handkerchief at my father, who looks inside for his means of protection. It's a gun, but it's all in pieces. As the story goes, the gangsters all found this dilemma hysterically funny. I guess even they could appreciate the irony of my father's predicament, and somehow, miraculously, decided not to hurt him, and even Alice got away unscathed. My sister Susan remembers Julius reassuring us that he would never have used the gun; it was just for show.

In return, John could tell my dad about how boxing saved his life, the day a Hartford, Connecticut, police lieutenant said, "Well, kid, you're pretty good with your hands, but if I have to see you again you're going to jail." John was getting into trouble constantly. He was perpetually angry, beating people up, and stealing. So the cop offered a few unappealing options: John could be tried in juvenile court or he could be sent off to the army. John was glum at these prospects. And then the cop had a brainstorm.

"You can box, you're angry enough; it should work." When John finally started training at Johnny Duke's gym, he was the only white kid, and a mere thirteen years old. Duke, chain-smoking and bedecked in cowboy boots, had a classical approach—when a white kid came to the gym, making his way as John did by enduring two long bus rides, he'd ask how much you weighed, how many fights you had behind you—and he'd immediately set up a sparring fight with a black guy. You'd be told to go work with Hector, whose dad was in prison for killing a white guy. If you came back the next day, that was impressive, although Hector still beat you up. Hector was *there* to beat you up. It was a carefully constructed trial by fire, and John endured it until *he* became the guy to beat.

"Jab, one-two. Jab, jab, blow to the body, blow to the head. There ya go," John is saying to me.

"The Punisher" is teaching me to crouch like a Ninja, slip and weave, keep my hands up, and send force up from my heavy legs into my middle and out through my arms, using my body in ways I never thought possible.

It's a surprise to feel so exhilarated by my own body and its abilities. *My body.* What a drag it's been—what a disappointment! Sometimes it just seemed like a necessary oversized backpack for my brain. My body has been, um . . . *sensitive.* Asthma and allergies as a teenager, lifelong irritable bowel syndrome that started at twenty-one after a particularly pernicious GI infection involving salmonella while living in New York City (not even after exotic travel), migraines and chronic headaches *forever.* Not to mention the dark cloak that swathed my whole family with a swirl of odd feelings, anxieties, phobias, and panic attacks. At times we've been like throwbacks to Freud's hysterical patients who couldn't lift an arm after seeing a snake or became obsessively aware of their tongues in their mouths.

So it's utterly new to feel my power, hear the propulsive sound of my own grunts, and experience such a delight in making this kind of physical contact. My body is bringing me *joy.* I'm also blinking desperately because my eyeballs are sweating. That's how *serious* an initiation I'm enduring—my *eyeballs* are affected.

I'd like to say straight out that I wish I'd found boxing earlier in my life, but my sisters and husband tell me that's a flaw in my psychology—happiness reminds me of sadness. There's an old joke: "*Doctor, doctor!*" a woman complains, "*I'm thirsty, my god, I'm thirsty . . . I'm soooooo thirsty! I'm dying of thirst!*" "*Ah,*" says the doctor, "*Take this water, you'll feel better.*" The woman drinks long and hard. "*Doctor, doctor! My god, I was sooooooo thirsty! I was dying of thirst!*" She goes on and on.

I think a lot about what might have been. When good things happen, I want to rewrite history and insert them earlier.

"So do you think you could really hit someone?" John talks without effort throughout our sessions. Two hundred pounds of fury, with a middleweight state championship belt rolled in the corner of a closet in his apartment above a New Haven bar, John could relieve me of my consciousness with one right cross. Of course he respectfully holds back. If he kills me, that's the end of the boxing lessons.

"Gee, I don't know if I could," I say, gasping and sputtering. This is like when the dentist is cheerfully inquiring where you went on vacation and your mouth is full of gleaming tools and cotton. You leak out a lone, wet, inaudible syllable, which satisfies him until his next ill-timed question.

I'm tightening my core, I'm keeping my knees bent, I'm bouncing back and forth on my feet, and I can barely breathe. I never participated in contact sports or athletics of any kind. I have not ever dominated a younger sibling, stood up to a bully, play-wrestled with a brother, or felt my own physical strength in any way. During particularly passionate fights with lovers, I have wiped a counter clear of a dish or two, and once I tore the buttons off a man's shirt, but I've never hit anyone, and the thought of it, well, the thought never occurred to me. It just wasn't an option. Like many women, I've experienced unwanted attention and wished I'd had the skills and courage to do something to protect myself. As far as being on the receiving end, my father slapped me when I objected to sharing a Whitman's Sampler box of chocolates with visiting relatives. It was the only time he hit me, but I'll never forget the shock of his hand zooming in.

Thwack! My glove makes contact with the punch-mitt on John's right hand. My god, it feels good. I do it again, remembering to snap my jab right back after I throw it. This is . . . it's . . . *thrilling*. I've never made such a profoundly clarifying sound with my fist before. To say that while I was growing up my family lacked a certain . . . *athleticism* . . . would be an understatement.

Although in the 1950s and 1960s President Kennedy put the nation on a physical fitness kick, in my home there was no concept of "fit," except as it applied to clothing, and because we didn't do sports, our obsessive interest in food made matters worse. My sister and I loved nothing more than to laze around watching television while consuming entire bags of Wise potato chips. I emptied boxes of animal crackers into large bowls and assembled them by size, eating the panther, the bear, and the lion first, and working my way expectantly up to the gorilla and hippo. My mother, though not the most inventive of cooks (I ate my first fresh mushroom in my twenties), could whip up a mean Duncan Hines sheet cake. Late at night my father would inhale a salami sandwich on rye with Gulden's Spicy Brown mustard over the kitchen sink. His traveling salesman tales were punctuated by detailed descriptions of the sumptuous meals at restaurants that he put on the expense account when he entertained the jobbers. "They had a spread, my daughters . . ." he intoned wistfully, while we listened with rapt attention to lurid tales of deli meats, chopped liver, cocktail shrimp, blintzes, and chocolate cheesecake.

Although my father had been a track star at Thomas Jefferson High, I never even saw him walk fast. My parents both seemed worn out. Newark's Weequahic High School had an award-winning basketball team, but I never knew anyone who played on it. (Philip Roth's Portnoy reminds us of the classic cheer of the era: *Ikey, Mikey, Jake, and Sam / We're the boys who eat no ham / We keep matzohs in our locker! Aye, Aye, aye, Weequahic High*!) In the 1940s, Roth and his buddies were still fleeing from anti-Semitic violence in the streets of Newark, especially perpetrated by kids from non-Jewish schools, and still Roth said, "I could no more smash a nose with a fist than fire a pistol into someone's heart."

I certainly never knew any boxers. In my Newark of the 1960s, I marched against the Vietnam War and considered myself something of a pacifist, just like the cooler-than-cool boys in high school I coveted, who professed a fierce pacifism when I quizzed them on fantasied scenarios of danger. *No, babe, I don't think I could defend you. Peace, baby*, they droned while trying to master Woody Guthrie chord progressions on acoustic guitars draped with embroidered straps.

"No one's got any balls anymore in this nation," John is saying as I continue pounding his punch mitt. "It's the worst for men—they get babied, and then they just look to be mothered."

Thug philosophy, I think, *simplistic but oddly compelling*.

By the hour's end, my sweat smells like a mixture of bitter oranges, aluminum, and old pastry. It could be a mixture of both our smells. Boxing is an intimate partner sport, one of the few that allows a man and woman to be physically involved without having sex. It is July, and John and I are sharing this physical intimacy in a small corner of the gym, where John has cleared away elliptical machines and treadmills with the deft push of one meaty hand. If my husband knew just how exciting I find this contact, he might want to pour molasses into my boxing gloves.

"Okay, baby," John beams. "Not too shabby." He knows I'm shot. "Now go hobble over to the water and take a break."

I walk over to the window ledge where I keep a collection of fluids—and encircle a bottle of vitamin water with two giant gloved hands, like a clumsy baby. Water spurts everywhere and dribbles down my chin. John laughs, and tells me not to worry; it's a dirty sport.

2 women

Bessie and Minnie Gordon are said to have been the first female boxing act, popular entertainers on the eastern seaboard vaudeville circuit. Their performance was billed as "bag punching and scientific act." The Gordon sisters' act is preserved in a two-minute film shot by Thomas Edison in 1901. The film is set on a theater stage with a painted backdrop of a French garden. In front of marble steps and a balcony, with trees in the background, two young women in flouncy knee-length skirts and sleeveless tops engage in a vigorous slugfest. Their curly blonde hair is kept in place with ribbons. They are wearing small boxing gloves tied to their wrists. Clearly they've had *some* boxing training, but they don't know how to protect themselves; you never see their hands up at their faces. The blows are thick, inside, fast, and sometimes flailing as their skirts blow around them as if strong weather is coming in. The slimmer woman, possibly the younger sister, spins around and her raised skirt reveals bloomers underneath. The heavier Gordon sister looks like a version of my Aunt Ettie, thick-waisted and clumsy. As she leans in to throw, her butt juts out. In the late nineteenth and early twentieth century, boxing was often done with bare-knuckles, and there are films and illustrations of those male pioneers, but this is the only time I have seen women of that era boxing. There is something surreal about this film. *They are wearing skirts, for one thing.*

I watch the film over and over. I want to identify with these women boxers, but I'm thinking of Aunt Ettie's upper arms shaking like loaves of bread, and her loud talk, issuing from a mouth full of brisket and potatoes. I don't want Aunt Ettie and women boxers to be in the same ring. I hate to admit this, but when I was a child I didn't like it when my relatives seemed "too Jewish." My grandmother's Yiddish words sounded garbled and phlegmy, like she should hold a hankie near her mouth when she spoke. Deep, strangled sounds came up from way down in her throat, always a warning, always a fear, always something to put out the sun in me. *Don't cut with scissors, it's Shabbas. Don't turn on lights. Don't ride your bicycle. Don't cook. Don't breathe. Don't laugh.* My maternal uncles were like a trio of typical immigrant workmen—Uncle Bobby was a butcher, Uncle Arthur was a tailor—if only Uncle Leon had been a baker or candlestick maker we would have had a full set—but he eventually moved to Texas, became some sort of salesman, and got a blonde shiksa wife (not a *shanda* for us, but definitely a novelty). I grew up pretty well assimilated, like the children of many second-generation immigrants. Roast chicken and challah adorned the table on Friday nights, once a year my father recited Kaddish for his younger brother who had died young of a burst appendix, but we belonged to no synagogue and my sisters and I did not attend Hebrew school. I did, however, attend my share of bar mitzvahs for the tribe of little boys who looked stiff in their suits and ties as they stuttered over Torah readings. A fountain pen was a common gift. *Today you are a man. So you should write about it?* Less frequently there would be a bat mitzvah for a girl, and I don't recall what those presents were.

I've never been very observant and it wasn't important for me to marry a Jewish man (and Scott isn't). When people tell me my appearance, my expressions, my identifications all code me as a "cultural Jew," it's always a bit of a surprise, but I easily dismiss it. Despite everything I knew to the contrary, I have never allowed that feature, of all the parts of a self, to seem too relevant. When people found my Jewishness a quirky factor in my love of boxing, this was suddenly a notion I couldn't push away so readily. It was as if boxing, a sport thought to be as far from Jewish experience as mayonnaise and white bread, exposed me as a Jew.

I too grew up thinking Jews were the pale scholars, heads buried in books, funny, warm, sensitive, but definitely not *physical.* They were not outdoorsy. Jules Feiffer spoke of his "great desire to grow up" because of his understanding that "adults did not have to take gym." A Jewish triathlon, as the joke goes, consists of "gin rummy, then contract bridge, followed by a nap." Woody Allen has infiltrated our collective psyche as the most influential Jewish comedian of the post–World War II era, and his persona and jokes highlight his physical vulnerability and meekness. With so many authors, comedians, and other celebrities aiding and abetting this portrayal of the unathletic Jew, it's no wonder I was shocked when I made some new Jewish friends who were busy naming their sailboats and buying second houses near ski resorts.

As far as religious practice, there were some major turnoffs. It was not lost on me as a child that men and women were separated in many synagogues. Women were not supposed to read the Torah, and coming from a family of readers, I found that maddening. I heard of a prayer that Orthodox men said daily, thanking god for not having made them female. Perhaps even more daunting were the messages of my more religious relatives, deeming any incomplete practice of Judaism to be a *shanda. How could you call yourself a Jew if you don't kiss the mezuzah or your way out! How can you not keep kosher? Why aren't you fasting on Yom Kippur?* Judaism seemed like a strange cult or club, offering highly prized tidbits that you could only taste if you agreed to eat the whole meal without hesitation.

Put me a boxing ring—*fine.*
Put me in a synagogue—*terror.*

When I started boxing I rented every boxing movie my local video store had in stock—including *The Harder They Fall, Champion*, all the *Rocky* movies, *Fat City, Body and Soul, Cinderella Man, The Great White Hope, Ali.* People often remember William Holden as *The Golden Boy*, Joe Bonaparte, son of Italian immigrant parents who desperately want him to continue with the violin and fear he will break his hand boxing. I was brought to tears when John showed me *Ring of Fire: The Emile Griffith Story* about the infamous 1962 fight in which rivals Emile Griffith and Benny Paret entered the ring for the world title bout. Paret had been taunting Griffith with a homosexual slur, a particularly provocative tactic at the time. As luck would have it, Paret died in the ring. John rewound the fight scene several times to teach me exactly what had happened; how this tragic accident prejudiced people against boxing for years, and how Griffith left the fight game and remained haunted for four decades afterwards by the death of his opponent. After this fight, the boxing commission instituted a rule for four ropes instead of three, so a fighter's head couldn't fall over the side and snap back the way it did for Paret.

I'd seen some of the films before, and they were exciting, but I couldn't actually . . . *relate*. For one thing, most boxing stories are about men. They portray a poor, oppressed guy who finds an outlet for his rage in a gym, like Benjamin Braddock, the underdog in *Cinderella Man*, fighting for all the immigrants, or the sweet but inarticulate brute of *Rocky*, who can't get out of his own way. Working in a meat factory in Philadelphia for a pittance, he earns extra cash as a debt collector. He grabs the chance for a nobody to become a somebody when heavyweight champion Apollo Creed's managers want to set up a match with a loser. But Rocky surprises them all, and the huge success of all five sequels suggests that his story resonates like the last chord of a great symphony, long after the musicians have packed up their instrument cases and headed home.

Many great authors (Ellison, Mailer, Hemingway, Oates) have been drawn to explore the more complex elements of boxing and its characters. Boxing has always had a colorful racial and class palette, and thrives on tribal identifications. It's been described as a mirror of society, and as my historywise coach says, like the development of jazz, baseball, and suburbia, its history would make an exciting college course in early Americana. Although it has taken a backseat to football and baseball, boxing is like a cold America can't get rid of; we can't shake our fascination with the primal pairing of two people willing to get into a ring, all eyes on them as we scream and boo, flirting with our own aggression. *Not me! Them! Yeah!*

Most boxing stories have a basic, predictable sequence: somebody needs to improve his economic status, has enough rage to fight, discovers boxing as an outlet, finds a mentor, and struggles to win, as we are led salivating from a safe distance to the longed-for moment of triumph. Sometimes, along the way, the arms of corruption beckon, and a boxer faces Faustian dilemmas.

New Yorker editor and author David Remnick says boxing is definitely a sport for the poor. Desperate times call for desperate measures, especially for those with few options. Today of course a flamboyant boxer like Floyd Mayweather, who literally tosses money into the air and conspicuously flashes gold jewelry, is far from desperate. His 2007 bout with Oscar DeLaHoya was a publicity event; neither fighter was willing to get hurt so they played nice, and although pay-per-view cable sales crested the $2 million mark, it made for a less than dramatic fight. My coach John says the guys today get spoiled and arrogant. "I wouldn't give 'em any money for a while," he says. "They've gotta be hungry."

Did I watch it? You bet!

I love the procession of the boxer. I click on HBO and boxers strut into the venues, often to the sonorous voice of Michael Buffer, who owns the phrase "*let's get ready to rumble*," which he stretches out like a limo, rolling his r's and making his voice louder and louder toward the conclusion of his famous phrase. If anybody says it in the media, Buffer gets a royalty. You can apply for a reward if you can document any unapproved use of the phrase.

Then—a man's face barely peeking out underneath a hooded robe, as if shrouded in ancient mysteries. Sometimes the man walks, sometimes he hops a little, warming up his muscles. Sometimes he looks down, as if into his own soul one last time before the battle. Sometimes you can see the glisten of a cross or other jewelry that is swiftly removed in the ring. All eyes are on him, the lights are flashing crisscross and sparkling, as people cheer and scream. The entourage hugs the boxer's body, flanking him like a flock of apostles, walking proud to support their man.

But it is not the team, it is the man. It is a perfect sport for a nonconformist, for a misfit, for a schizoid type. Every boxing match is a narcissist's dream; you are the center of your drama, sharing the stage with another boxer who is your necessary mirror and who is in your way.

The bell rings and the boxers retire to their corners. Men hop in ready to tend their hero. Often, at least three men are touching the boxer all at once, wiping his face down with Vaseline, pouring water on his head, offering him tiny sips from a bottle, repairing cuts, pressing down a swollen cheek or eye with a piece of steel that looks like a miniature iron. It's called "unswell." You can get one from the Everlast catalog, a company founded in 1910 by Russian-Jewish immigrant Jack Golomb. The boxer, in a suspended state until the next bell, stares beyond his coaches as they warn, "*Use your right more! Don't be afraid of him! What are you doing? What did we talk about! Remember what I told you—use your right! This is nothing, he's nothing! You're the champ, c'mon, what are you doing? That's right, baby, just keep doing what you're doing.*"

And if the corner men are Spanish, Russian, Latvian? No problem. Their words are translated. Everything is mic-ed so our curiosity can be fed. "*Move that head! Move out! All right? All right?*

Stay relaxed, nice and loose. One, two, three, get out! Pop that jab out! You hear me? He's waiting for you! Block his punches! You got it now so that whenever you fight, he reacts. Don't let him out."

As part of my training, I returned to some of the boxing movies I'd seen, but not just for the drama. I used to fast-forward through the fight sequences; now I was rewinding to study the punches and combinations.

Female boxing movies were harder to find. I watched *Million Dollar Baby* for the second time with different eyes. Billie the Blue Bear, who cripples Maggie Fitzgerald in their bout, was played by professional fighter Lucia Rijker. Rijker was born and raised in Amsterdam, is a practicing Buddhist, the complete opposite of the sadistic and menacing bully she plays in the film, and one of the strongest and most beautiful women I have ever seen. (Interestingly, the scene of Billie the Bear hitting Maggie appalled many viewers and, in truth, it would never occur in regulated boxing—a blow when a fighter's back is turned just wouldn't happen and, if it did, that dirty fighter would never fight again.) In a dusty back section of my video store I found the documentary *Shadow Boxers*, which follows Rijker training at a camp with all men. Rijker says she doesn't fight with anger or because of anger. "I have a job to do," she says, "and they're just in my way." It's hard for Rijker to get fights—she's too good and no one wants to fight her. It's a conundrum shared by many women fighters—there just aren't enough of them who are willing to throw in with the best.

The women's stories, while not as plentiful, also have obvious elements of adversity and triumph. Laila Ali, who as the daughter of Muhammad Ali you'd imagine would have all the access and privileges to assure her a good life, was an acting-out adolescent who stole, got into fights, felt ignored at home, and wound up in a juvenile detention center. Her modest goal for many years was to open a nail salon. When she became a successful boxer, she jumped into the hero's journey that captivates us. Laila Ali says she loves "the give-and-take" of boxing, "anticipating a punch before it's thrown." "I see the footwork," she says, "the motion, the dance in my dreams. I love the subtle play between defense and offense, jabbing and ducking, moving ahead, maintaining position, giving ground, gaining momentum." Watching *Daddy's Girl*, a documentary about her life, I am fascinated by her strength and beauty; she's a goddess. While speaking at a women's prison, she hands out her autobiography *Reach!* to the younger girls.

"Go after your dreams," she tells them, their faces skeptical, sullen. "Be fearless."

Women's boxing got professional acknowledgment in the 1970s. Today there are more than seven hundred professional women boxers, with the ranks of amateurs growing all the time, and women are finally going to be able to compete in boxing at the 2012 Olympics. Still, women make less money boxing than men. A match that might bring a man $5000 for the night may bring the woman only $1200.

But when it's a woman being escorted into the ring I feel a particularly special thrill. She's been admitted into the club; she's broken through the barriers. The smoke clears, and it's like the Incredible Hulk rips open a flimsy shirt to reveal spectacular muscles. Or breasts.

"Women are actually better students of boxing," John once said to me while we were training. "They listen better, and because they realize they don't have brute strength on their side, they approach it in a much more cerebral fashion than men do. One time in Colorado Springs, this boxing expert guy, some PhD . . . was pontificating on the merits of female boxers—the challenge was 'women aren't as strong and boxing is very physical so you have to train them the right way' blah, blah, blah—so you should have them get in the ring and 'wrestle a bit' first! I said 'do you prefer Jell-o or pudding—typically Jell-o is easier to clean up!' Stupidest thing I ever heard. So the guy says no, I meant to make their upper bodies stronger. All my women can box. But there are interesting differences. Men are thinking how can I punch through this guy's gloves, whereas women are thinking how can I get around them."

It was true. All I could think of when I boxed was: John was in my way. Constantly. I kept imagining deft combinations where I could finally, triumphantly, get at his chin with an uppercut, put my left hook up high enough to crest his right arm and get him on the side of the head, and so on. I tried to deliver body blows from too great a distance. They were ineffective; I couldn't get inside. He was fast, he was powerful. What could I do?

"That was the same exhibition where the jerk said another crazy thing," John went on. "They had a heavybag hooked up to a monitor that measures power and the coaches had a demo with the top-ranked boxers . . . I was encouraged to step up and be part of the demo. A guy next to me was this old black trainer, great guy, I'd worked with him, and he's yelling 'throw your hip into it!' Then the PhD guy again chimes in and says, 'there really have been no correlating studies that suggest that rotating the hip will apply any more power to a punch.' And this ancient black trainer who's seen it all, shouts out, 'Nigger, shut up! Shut the fuck up! How many fighters you ever trained!' That shut him up."

"Also," John added, "women's bodies have a lower site of gravity, more weight. Those hips, they're good for this." His bear paw/punch mitt motioned toward my lower half.

Aaaahhhh, yes. My brains are useful here, as are my Slavic legs. I have found my place in the universe.

Women are better students of boxing. Along with being nonathletic, all I'd heard all my life was that men were stronger than women. Men were stronger than women, Jews didn't ski; the beliefs just went on and on. John hadn't said anything about women's innate strength; he said we were better students. Of course you'd hear, too, that women thought too much, felt too much; people still mentioned it in conversations about a woman being president. It was still in the collective consciousness that a woman might be unreliable. But John said the intensity was a plus. He also said that while men pictured the face of a bully they longed to hit, women saw no one face; instead they experienced a general feeling of empowerment. This difference proved true of every male and female boxer I ever met. One woman said boxing actually made her feel more feminine.

When I met Sue, a thirty-year-old women's studies teacher who trains with John, she said it made her feel sexier and more at peace with her curvy plus-size body. She also kickboxes with him, and she loves being able to put "my short, heavy leg up to his shoulder." Although Sue bought herself black handwraps because they look tougher, she doesn't want to hit or spar with John, ever; he is "too much like a cuddly teddy bear" to her, and a surrogate brother. "Father figure?" she asked, surprised. "How could that be? He's not that old!" So they stay with the punch mitts.

A match can be over in a flash—all the preparation, all the hopes, all the training, all the encouragement, all the hype and promotion. In the 2007 Alfonso Gomez–Arturo "Thunder" Gatti fight, Gatti was down after a brief two minutes. Once those moments are over, the interviewers swarm, microphones stuck in exhausted faces, millions of questions fired, and the boxer, sweat dripping, struggles to respond. There is mostly humility. Sometimes they are cocky. The loser is interrogated, too. "What happened? What do you think went wrong?"

The ones who get knocked out, like Gatti in this fight, often deny it.

"What? What do you mean? I didn't get knocked out! That's crazy!"

John tells me it's because they literally don't remember anything after the blow.

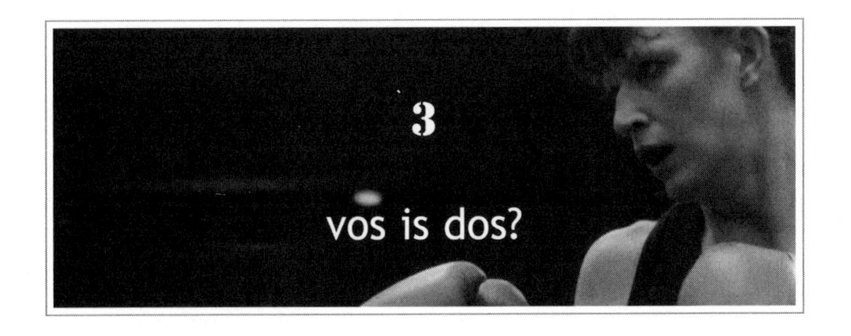

By the fourth lesson with John, I was dreaming punches. One morning my husband grabbed my hand, which had been moving automatically in my sleep. Both hands had been going back and forth. We fell back asleep with our hands entwined, but my husband said I was still trying to move my fists. Soon after that I met Joan, a woman in her late fifties who told me that, after two years of boxing with John, her husband reached over to gently fix her hair and her hands went up reflexively.

"What does Scott think about all this?" John asked me once.

"Um, I guess he's supportive . . . but he wonders where it's all going."

John was acutely aware that the men in the lives of his women clients were not always so understanding. Maybe that's why he was asking about Scott. But it's not like I was Maggie Fitzgerald in *Million Dollar Baby*. I wasn't battling for recognition, and no one was standing in my way. People looked startled when they heard I was boxing. "You?" they'd say. *Why are you so shocked?* I wanted to ask, *Is it because I'm older? Because I'm not trim and fit? Because I'm a woman?* Somehow the aggression or intensity required to hit was understandable coming from a man. But, with a woman, it was an anomaly. Why on earth would a woman want to punch? Or be hit?

Or was it something else altogether that people were thinking?

Maybe they don't think my profession fits with the sport. *You're a therapist*, they scold, as if reminding me that in choosing my career I was to be denied the physical plane altogether, a brain suspended in a tank like in a 1950s science-fiction movie.

You're not supposed to be aggressive, right? Aren't you supposed to have it all analyzed and sublimated?

Yeah, right. There's nothing like donning boxing gloves and headgear to make you face your own competitiveness, rage, and desire for dominance. My inclinations were shocking.

People ask me—do your patients know? Some do because I've referred them for boxing lessons to help them feel their own physical power and competence. Therapists fall into two groups: those who pretend that their patients know nothing personal about them and struggle to keep it that way. They won't give opinions, and they won't tell you where they're going on vacation. You've already guessed which group I'm in. The mystery therapists may be perfectly helpful therapists; they just don't roll that way. But there are the inevitable clues emanating from their faces and their walls, whether their humor is direct, sardonic, or missing altogether; whether their offices are adorned with Klee prints and tasteful soapstone sculptures or a just a dusty row of crookedly hung diplomas; whether they are outfitted in blazers and chinos or Flax clothing and chunky jewelry; and whether the car sitting in the therapist's space is a Prius with a Think Globally, Act Locally sticker or a brand-new Saab with a ski rack.

Being a boxer is a bit like being part of a sexual minority—we take pleasure in something many people don't understand and feel compelled to judge us for—but sometimes when I talk about boxing, a surprising number of people, both women and men, begin to imagine themselves with boxing gloves on. I recognize the look. Their innocent eyes widen. They start talking about how they did five minutes of kickboxing in an aerobics class once.

They're intrigued . . . and then they're curious . . . and then, in almost a whisper: *So where did you say you do this?*

If boxing is also a sport for the poor, as Remnick says, it is a sport about ethnic minorities and ethnic pride—Irish, Italian, African American, Mexican, and so on. Joyce Carol Oates, in her amazing book *On Boxing*, says the sport is the story of black men, but she wrote this before the influx of Hispanics and Slavs.

"John," I asked after finding the film of the Gordon sisters boxing, "were there any Jewish boxers?"

"Absolutely there were Jewish boxers—Benny Leonard, Al "Bummy" Davis, Abe Attell, Barney Ross, "Slapsie" Maxie Rosenbloom. In 1930, there were six Jewish champions. Sometimes they took Irish names, can you imagine—like Mushy Callahan. Light welterweight. His real name was Moische Schneir. And they were all very good, too. And if you go way back—Daniel Mendoza in Britain. Bare-knuckle boxer. He even wrote a memoir. There's a young guy now, Dimitri-something . . . there's an article about him in *Ring* Magazine. I think he's Orthodox, even."

Wow. Hearing those names was disorienting. Although I grew up hearing the names of great boxers—Dempsey, Graciano, Ali, Tyson, Frazier, and Foreman, I hadn't heard these—the ones who sounded like relatives. Strong tough *Jews*? *Boxers*?

"Why would they take Irish names?" I asked.

"Why do you think, brainy girl? Don't you know anything about your people?" He'd been calling out punches and stopped moving in circles to glare at me.

"Oh, of course. They were trying to be accepted." I felt like an idiot.

There are these odd and embarrassing blips in my knowledge. My worst subjects in the game of Trivial Pursuit are geography and history. I've often wanted to go back to school . . . *grade school*. Oh, to have another chance at the basic facts of the world. Maps and wars and algebra and the finer points of grammar.

My hometown of Newark has a seaport that is one of the largest in the country, but I never knew that. We were landlocked, in stacked apartments, each a mirror image of the other, tiny bedrooms, barely an eat-in kitchen, linoleum on the floors, and a mezuzah on the doorway, often painted five times over so that it seemed as plain as a hinge, a faded wooden bulge that meant nothing to us kids except that it came with the apartments, like wainscoting or molding. The Weequahic section was full of second- and third-generation Jews who had made it out of Brooklyn, yet we lived mostly inside our four rooms, with very little attachment to community or extended family. It was my father who had the most connection to the *outside* world, through his travels, and it was my father who separated my mother from her sisters and brothers, calling them peasants, and denigrating her past. Perhaps after such profound uprooting she felt safest inside our apartment, and did not fight this characterization.

Where I *came* from, that is—who and what were my ancestors—was a foggy, spotty tale kept at a distance from the present. There was no active conspiracy to bury facts; they were just deemed threatening to the tremendous pressure to assimilate and be like everybody else. Concentration camps? Pogroms? *Way back. Too horrible. Don't think about that. Don't ask Mommy to ask Grandma—you'll upset them both.*

Part of where my parents came from was the terrain of immigrant communities in U.S. cities. It's hard for us to imagine the conditions of such neighborhoods—overcrowding, bathrooms in hallways, filthy coal stoves, poor sanitation in the streets. In parts of New York, cattle were herded through the streets toward the slaughterhouse, right in front of your tenement stoop. Children were often forced to work in shops and died young, their parents toiling fourteen to sixteen hours a day in factory sweatshops. When I first heard of Eugene O'Neill's play, *The Iceman Cometh*, I thought the iceman was a prehistoric monster. In 1926, an iceman would deliver chopped ice to your apartment for ten cents. Streets were filled with peddlers, vendors, and pushcarts. Most of life was lived out on the streets, to escape the overcrowding inside the tenements.

In the 1920s, Jewish immigrants and children of immigrants were seeking to become part of mainstream American culture.

Boxing was one of the few ways to improve your economic situation. It was said that "fast feet and fast hands were the best ticket out of the ghetto." Jewish boxers, like other struggling immigrant groups, fought to put meat and potatoes on the table (or should I say brisket and latkes). There were a few star football players, too—like Benny Friedman, ace quarterback with the New York Giants from 1929 to 1931. He was the son of working-class Orthodox immigrants from Russia.

John had lit the flame for me—I was curious—and I found that between 1910 and 1940, *one-third of all boxers were Jewish.* At one point, Jews held three titles simultaneously. Proportionately, it was an enormous number, and a direct result of the huge migration of Jews from Europe in the late nineteenth century and through the first three decades of the twentieth century. Escaping their countries, or driven from them, Jews wound up in the poorest and most crowded ghetto neighborhoods in the cities. Penniless, speaking no English, the largest percentage of immigrants landed at Ellis Island and moved into the Lower East Side of Manhattan.

When these transplanted Jews found that they could not walk through the streets of New York wearing a yarmulke without being threatened, they were appalled to again be dealing with anti-Semitism. Not surprising then to read that the *Thesaurus of the Yiddish Language* lists 392 synonyms for the word "hit," which most likely come from being on the receiving end and then learning how to fight back. *K'nack, patch, tzettle, zet, diokh, hak,* to name a few.

Throughout history, Jews have been threatened, chased, bullied, derided, and of course one cannot think about Jewish toughness without picturing its complete opposite: those haunting images of emaciated bodies in concentration camps, horrific helplessness, when we were systematically starved and killed in an attempt to eliminate us altogether.

Paul Breines wrote *Tough Jews* in 1990 to "present a survey of general Jewish history as a history of tough Jews, as against the obvious and not altogether mistaken assumption that Jewish history is largely a story of Jewish victimization." The systematic destruction of the ancient Jewish state and, later, the holocaust contributed to the image of the Jews making "a culture of meekness, physical frailty, and gentleness, a pale, slouched identity." The mistaken notion, he says, is "the assumption . . . that Jews are by *nature* or by some religious or racial *essence* gentle or weak."

I grew up hearing the oft-repeated question: "Why didn't they rise up and fight back? There were so many of them." As if this entire group of people was complicit in its own destruction. It haunted me. Then the balm of scholar Walter Laqueur's words removed some of the sting: it is "ahistorical, if not unethical and indecent, to pass judgment of the behavior of persons in the most extreme peril for their lives . . . from the vantage point of the present."

Edward Zwick's 2009 film *Defiance*, the story of the courageous Bielski brothers, Jews who saved other Jews in a partisan resistance movement, evoked considerable fascination with its challenge to the cultural record of tales of utter helplessness and victimhood.

But the ideas and images of a so-called Jewish Identity are constantly being mixed together, and one cannot make any sweeping assertions about the hugely complex issues of the Holocaust. Strong or timid, bookish or physical, many Jewish men recall being cautioned not to play baseball as children for fear they would get hurt. I recently asked Stephen Acunto, founder along with Rocky Marciano of the *American Association for the Improvement of Boxing*, what he thought Jewish boxers brought to the sport. "They didn't want to get hurt, you see, so they were the best at defense." He paused. "And of course they were smart." Former *Boxing Digest* editor Hank Kaplan wrote that "Jews as boxers sounds like a contradiction in terms." He had the same picture of Jews as gentle folk who used their humor and brains to resolve differences, rather than their fists. I guess Kaplan wasn't thinking of my father's buddies in Murder, Inc., but those were such extremes, anyway. Besides, it was hard to admire extortion, murder, and brute force.

When the Jewish boxers stepped into the ring, they were fighting the stereotype of Jews as weaklings and cowards. Champion Benny Leonard's mother wept at his first black eye, but when he brought home his first winnings, she had to acknowledge that it was better than working in a sweatshop. This is how boxing helped bring the East European Jewish immigrants and their children into something more mainstream in America. In 1917, Benny Leonard won the lightweight championship of the world and kept the title until 1925.

Budd Schulberg said of watching Leonard: "To see him climb in the ring sporting the six-pointed star on his fighting trunks was to anticipate sweet revenge for all the bloody noses, split lips and mocking laughter at pale little Jewish boys who had run the neighborhood gauntlet."

When famed boxer Barney (Beryl Rasofsky) Ross first stepped into Kid Howard's small gym on the South Side of Chicago, he was a scrawny fifteen-year-old suffering from malnutrition. When they fought, Jewish boxers often proudly wore the Star of David on their trunks. "My Yiddishe Mama" was played as Barney Ross entered the ring.

During this Golden Age of Boxing, the amount of boxing activity was remarkable. Most fighters averaged at least one fight a month—compare this to today's professional boxers averaging fewer than six fights a year.

As more economic opportunities opened up, boxing's torch was taken up by the Irish, Italians, African Americans, and Hispanics. As much as boxing has pitted ethnic groups against each other, it has also presented rare opportunities for minorities to advance. It's hard to feel just one way about this.

The last Jewish champ was Mike "the Jewish Bomber" Rossman, who held the light heavyweight crown in the late 1970s. Mike's father was actually Italian, but he chose to go by his mother's maiden name. He turned pro at the age of seventeen and had to fight illegally because he was underage for professional boxing, but he won twenty-two bouts in a row.

In the twenty-first century, from Brooklyn by way of Ukraine, and to the accompaniment of a live Klezmer band or the sounds of Chassidic rapper Matisyahu, twenty-five-year-old Dmitriy Salita strides into the ring. He's an orthodox Jew with an undefeated record. He studies with a Lubavitcher rabbi and no amount of money would make him fight on the Sabbath. Somehow he makes it all fit together.

Dmitriy has said, "I enjoy being different. People are surprised at how good the white Jewish kid is, surprised that I can fight. I take that as a compliment."

Dat's vos is dos, Grandma. Images of Jewish toughness—that's what I was craving; of course I didn't notice the ones that had been there all along. I think you must have had some of it when you fled the pogroms in Poland and boarded the ship *Roussillon* from the shtetl Ciechanow and landed at Ellis Island, although you might not have felt very strong. You were only twenty-eight years old. My mother was with you, and she was eight, along with her older sister, my Aunt Esther. At Ellis Island, an abandoned ammunitions dump, you followed the others, carrying bedrolls, blankets, baskets, babies. Many days 12,000 people were processed. You faced an assembly line of immigration officials, endured a brusque and humiliating physical exam. Your mother-in-law, wearing a sign marked "senility," was somehow let in, although she failed the intelligence test. At the registration, like a day of judgment, you were asked your name, your place of birth, your destination, how much money you had, whether you were ever in jail or were ever an anarchist. You were met by relatives from Brooklyn, maybe your husband Isadore, who had come over first, like many of the men. Finally, exhausted, you boarded the ferry to Manhattan Island, which must have looked like heaven, with the skyscrapers reaching into the clouds.

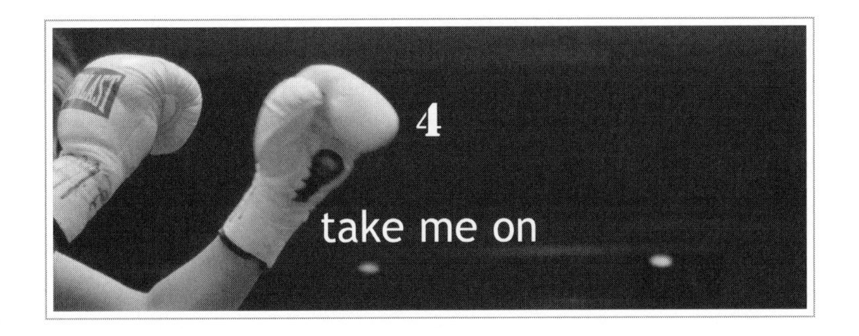

4 take me on

I found my boxing coach because of a story in an American Association of Retired Persons (AARP) newsletter. I was still barely getting used to the fact that I received such a document. Wasn't it just yesterday I had been a promiscuous young rock'n roller? I had gone to "happenings" and "be-ins" in the 1960s, my first boyfriend warned me he would be joining the revolution someday while intensely applying hickeys to my neck as we watched episodes of *The Fugitive*, but now I was, oh god, a nice lady who was riding the same bus as the other ladies, or had just come out of a discount store, or was checking out books at the library; we were part of a great mass of undistinguished, decent, average people. I was being lassoed in, rounded up with a huge undifferentiating net.

And we all got the AARP bulletin.

"Women Boxers, Middle-Aged, Fearless." Right on the front page. There they were, bedecked in boxing shorts and sport bras, their fists encased in leather boxing gloves, their expressions happy and strong. I scanned the text excitedly. These were local women who were working with a real boxer. His name was John. He was training them to box like he trained men. It wasn't kickboxing, it wasn't Tae-Bo; it was serious boxing. They said it was an intense workout and a lot of fun. I knew a little about it because I'd had an injury that led me to a physical therapist who let me put on some gloves.

John, a former boxer himself, was practicing this magic at a gym in my very own town. Things like this didn't happen. The proximity and possibility were irresistible. I pictured Hilary Swank in *Million Dollar Baby*, hounding Clint Eastwood in a seedy gym to "take her on." Her character, Maggie Fitzgerald, like many other boxing heroes, had nothing in her life that brought her any success or gratification. Boxing was her only chance; she was desperate. Was I desperate? Boxing wouldn't be taking me out of a poor neighborhood or an abusive relationship, nor was I needing such rescue. It wouldn't make me any money. What I did feel was lonely and disconnected. I did not feel a sense of vitality. The country was having one long, rapturous, and unending love affair with youth, and I felt sour, bitter, and dry. I approached my naked body in the mirror cautiously, like a wolf sizing up its prey, eyes narrowed, not in lustful need for food, but in terror . . . and then, it could only be confronted in sections, like a cafeteria plate (peas separated from mashed potatoes), as each day brought a new pocket of dimpled and sagging flesh. I turned the bathroom fan *off* when I showered, letting the steam create a mercifully diffuse and hazy reflection in the mirror. While reaching for the toothpaste, I might glimpse just the delicate curve of an underarm, the slight indentation of a waist, and retain the sensuous image of an Impressionist painting.

I looked at the article at least once every week, turning the stone, as if I were willing myself into the photographs, imagining myself standing tall and tough with the other women. There are many stones left unturned in the course of a lifetime, but there are also those you do pick up, peer at intently, caress, maybe even sniff a bit, the way animals and babies do, and then rub against the side of your face—just to see how they feel. The stones are often inconsistent with your sense of identity, and with others' opinions of you. And then the unrehearsed words pop inexplicably out of your mouth, and a suddenly articulated desire leads you to an unexpected place. It happens when you follow a hunch, when you purchase a box of art supplies although you've never painted, when you decide to train for a marathon at an advanced age, when you go back to school to study the most arcane, least-financially profitable pursuit, like the migration of butterflies or the bisexual proclivities of bonobo chimpanzees. This is when you are picking up the weird stones.

I thought of trying to contact the women from the pictures, but I never did. Eventually I resolved to find this mysterious "John." I imagined calling him "boss" and eagerly pounding a speedbag while he looked on, skeptical but ultimately proud as a parent of my determination.

Once I found my nerve, I had to contain my enthusiasm for a while, because John the boxing coach was elusive. I left several eager messages on a cellphone number reluctantly provided by a young woman at Fit World where he worked, her voice tightly suspicious and protective. I wondered if they all could hear from *my* voice that I was old and decrepit.

Maybe this was all just an oddball notion, the dream of another person altogether. What was I thinking? Boxing coach! I should just enjoy my languid walks in the woods with my husband, living through our dogs' ecstatic and fearless romps. Slow, rapturous kayak trips down gentle rivers were adding a lovely dimension to our lives. The whole boxing thing was not looking promising, and I might just as easily have given it up, until finally one day I saw an unfamiliar email address in my in-box.

"Hey there. I'm in Paris but I'll be back in two weeks. Give me a call and we'll meet when I get back and we'll talk about boxing."

Paris? Teaching boxing must be lucrative. Or was there some big French boxing match going on?

"The boxing coach got back to me!" I excitedly told Scott.

"Ah. Great," he said.

❖

When you are first joining, a gym is like a sales convention. Smiles are broad, handshakes are extended, there's a sexy vibe in the air. Fit World, however, was a seriously no-frills operation and offered no such welcome. This was where I met John, at his last job before he opened his own club.

I had dressed for a possible workout in case John wanted to "check me out" right away, to see if I had any potential—loose-fitting drawstring pants, running shoes, and a tank top, nothing special. The key element was my trusty sports bra made like a suspension bridge that promised to keep my large chest from bouncing and jiggling.

"I'm looking for John." Up close now, I could see that the "girl" on the phone had penciled-in slashes for eyebrows, was considerably older than I had imagined, and looked like a Las Vegas showgirl stricken with melancholia. She was stacking a pile of limp-looking power bars.

"Oh, you must be Bernie. He's in his office."

She pointed toward a small room in the middle of the club.

The door to John's office was open. He was removing long yellow straps from the hands of a tall, handsome guy with rippling six-pack abs. This was it; I had stepped into the famous moment of films and anecdotes of men. A few elements were missing, of course. I was not a hungry inner-city youth looking for a way out. The room was not smoke-filled, and there were no beautiful dames hanging around. Instead, I was the one female, a decidedly unathletic one, who got the AARP bulletin.

"That's right, baby," John was saying, "I've been teaching nice smart people for twenty years to smash things and no one has gone crazy."

John called everyone "baby."

I tried to find a spot near the wall. My longed-for coach looked like a Mafia hit man, burly, thick-necked, tough, and intimidating, as if any minute he'd pull out an envelope full of cash to buy my silence. My mother and I often watched gangster movies that reminded us of my father (you'd think he was a highly employed character actor), and all Edward G. Robinson roles made us think of him, oppressed, sullen, prone to rages and random acts of generosity. We never said aloud "Daddy," but the thrill of recognition was in the air. She smoked her Kents, I ate Cracker Jacks.

When I later saw a photograph of boxer Barney Ross, he looked a lot like my father and a lot like Edward G. Robinson. Once inside John's office, I was concocting images of men, gamblers, corruption, careless slaps, and humiliation, things that were telescoped on my own father's face—a certain slipperiness to their mouths, a wet cigar. Shimmers of recognition were flickering at the edges of everything in boxing and I just kept following the sparks.

My father was addicted to the racetrack, and knew some shady characters. He and Barney Ross. They both appear in photographs in tilted fedoras, white suits, looking dapper, up for anything, and a bit nuts. Although after certain "good days" at the track in Saratoga Springs, Daddy treated us all to an expensive dinner at the Wishing Well, where I always ordered a Shirley Temple, shrimp cocktail, and lamb chops, suspicions of major financial losses caused by gambling hovered in the air throughout our lives. I remember the phrase: "*When my ship comes in . . .*"

When Barney Ross wasn't boxing, he was an unlucky gambler who couldn't pick a winner, but he loved the track. Not surprisingly, there's always been a link between gambling and professional boxing, and organized crime has long been involved in the sport. John L. Sullivan's bid for the championship in 1892 was financed by a Chicago organized crime boss. Criminal involvement has sometimes taken the form of gambling syndicates asking a boxer to "throw" a fight—lose a match deliberately. The Faustian dilemma. Primo Canera, who boxed during the early 1930s and was a favorite of my father's, was under the control of an American crime syndicate, and fighter Jake "Raging Bull" La Motta threw a fight against Billy Fox after he was unable to obtain a title bout without the consent of the mob.

Controversy continued through the 1970s, 1980s, and 1990s over many of the fights organized by promoter Don King, who himself has a criminal record.

My father's "acquaintances" in Murder, Inc. probably included Bugsy Siegel and Meyer Lansky. Italian American gangsters Charles "Lucky" Luciano and Johnny Torrio, the former boss of the Chicago Outfit and mentor of New York native Al Capone, allied themselves, and Murder, Inc. was a group of men who would be on call 24/7 to handle any "problems" that afflicted la Cosa Nostra. Murder, Inc. originally was a group of mostly Jewish-American hit men from the Brownsville section of Brooklyn. Its headquarters was next door to a "Socony" gas station on Stone and Sutter avenues, where the members proved highly effective in keeping everyone in line. They'd be the ones to eliminate problems such as eyewitnesses and reluctant payers. They also fulfilled most murder contracts. Siegel and Lansky had moved on to other, larger pastures, and control over Murder, Inc. was ceded to Louis "Lepke" Buchalter and Albert Anastasia (known in underworld circles as "The Mad Hatter" and, more ominously, "The Lord High Executioner"). The infamous Frankie Carbo worked for Lepke and established himself as "The Czar of Boxing." The Mafia, via Anastasia and Carbo and Carbo's partner, Mafioso Blinky Palermo, took over the sport of boxing and manipulated the odds and fixed the fights to aid their bookie operations. Carbo ran New York boxing, which was *the* greatest boxing center, from his New York bookie operation until the 1960s, when he and Palermo were convicted and sentenced to prison.

The rise of Jewish gangsters was not seen as such a happy development to many, but nevertheless, as Breines says in *Tough Jews*, it "played a significant role in the gradual integration of Jews into American society." It was proof that if the Irish and Italians could get out of the tenements and gain power through crime, so could the Jews. Hearing some of the gangster's names (Irving Knadles Nitzberg, Dutch Schultz, Bugsy Siegel, Gyp the Blood,

Dopey Benny Fein, Arnold Rothstein, Gurrah Shapiro, etc.) evoked an odd thrill of recognition, like hearing the names of the Jewish boxers.

"I think that people are taught to be timid," John was saying. "Everyone feels timid is the way to go and when you give them a chance to push it, do something out of the box, it feels really good, but the first thought when not being timid is: this is wrong."

Timid. That sounded like me in relation to my body. The tall guy nodded, admiring John's words, and started to walk out, brushing past me as if I was not really there. John motioned me to the chair and I sat down across from him while he made a few notes on a yellow lined pad.

"So what interests you about boxing?" John asked, not yet making eye contact.

I leaned forward, onto a desk littered with papers, *Ring* magazines, post-it notes, and a stack of books about the French Revolution.

The Paris connection?

I launched into my spiel, full of Hilary Swank large-toothed enthusiasm—never athletic, found Jacob, a trainer at another gym (I didn't call him a physical therapist—that would have marred the illusion of my fitness), discovered boxing, love it so much! I said nothing about my fears, my phobias, my concerns about injury or lack of competence in order to sell myself as tough, or at least potentially tough, otherwise he wouldn't waste his time with me. "There's just something about it . . ." My voice trailed off. John looked huge, larger than life, expansive, and I felt small and unformed.

"Well, listen, it is the greatest secret, the best workout. I don't trust yoga people. Too tight, too inward. So you can stretch your leg in back of your head; I'm not impressed! Boxing forces you to face your fears. But I'm not looking for the next champion, I gotta tell ya, I'm kind of winding down. And I'm the best-kept secret around town. You found me though." He talked fast.

"It wasn't so easy," I smiled.

"Well, you were persistent and I liked that." Now his eyes met mine and rested there. He leaned back in his chair.

Movie-watching had paid off. All of it.

John didn't try me out that day; instead we scheduled for later that week, and when I returned I was happy that two kayaks were still loaded on top of my Subaru. I hoped he could see them through the gym window, and see what a jock I was.

John looked at the inner gloves I was using with the punching gloves in my sessions with Jacob, fingerless items that protected your knuckles with a cushiony material.

"Hmmm, interesting," he said. There were bright yellow straps coiled in the corner, the kind he used to wrap the guy's hands in his office. These wraps have a colorful history. The early Greek boxers protected their hands and wrists by wrapping them with thin strips of leather. Later, as the Romans modified boxing to become a more bloody and spectacular entertainment, they included heavier leather for the wraps and even metal studs. This all formed a "cestus" that led to another sinister weapon—the "myrmex" (limb piercer). Often, slaves or gladiators were forced to fight each other to the death.

It was to be the last day I'd use my padded devices on sale from Sports Authority. It was on to the Roman arena for me!

"C'mere," John said, "let me wrap you."

I stuck out my hand.

"Nope. Right hand first. It's my quirk."

He began to coil the long yellow strap around my wrist several times and then through my fingers. I was being swaddled, and it felt wonderful. A sudden image of Orthodox men wrapping *tefillin* popped into my mind. They wrap themselves in a careful ritual in order to be ready to pray. Perhaps the wrapping itself is a kind of prayer. My prayer—*Please let me not look utterly foolish* —was certainly unorthodox, and most likely a *shanda.*

"Okay, let's see. Lemme show you the basic stance. Stand next to me and look in the mirror."

Oh no, a giant mirror. I tried to ignore how clumsy and fat I looked and focused on my new teacher's words.

"The jab is your bread-and-butter punch," John said, thrusting his left hand into the air with a short, defiant burst. "It's a way to establish your range, see what's out there. And it sets you up for the right cross."

"You mean the right jab?"

"There *is* no right jab. What are you talking about?"

"Oh, I thought, well, the other trainer said . . ."

"This is what kills me about those typical gym trainers. They don't know anything about boxing." John looked impatient.

"He didn't mean . . . he always admitted his lack of knowledge."

"Well, then you were lucky; you got a good human being there."

John held up two pairs of gloves, pink and white, offering me a choice.

"White! I'm not a pink sort of girl." All of a sudden I was butch; all memories of scraping my knees in the shallow end of the lake at summer camp had disappeared.

John fitted my hands into the gloves, holding them against his sturdy body. "Okay, jab. Jab, one two. Jab. Jab, Jab. C'mon, snap it back."

I pushed at the air.

"Don't push! Snap it! Use your hips! Put your body into it!" He walked over to the corner to a plastic box with colored buttons atop it and pressed down.

A brittle piercing sound ripped the air, and I jumped like Betty Boop fleeing a mouse.

"Hey, I thought you had some experience boxing." He smirked and shook his head.

Now he'd never take me on. Yes, it was the bell, the clang, the buzzer, the call to action.

"A lot of phrases come from boxing," John said, releasing an impressive cascade of information. "Low blow, hitting below the belt, sucker punch, calling the fight, throw in the towel, the gloves are off, punching your weight, give it your best shot—but, guess what? Saved by the bell—everybody thinks that's from boxing, but it's not! It was about how wealthy people were buried with these strings a really long time ago. People were terrified they might be buried alive; if you were secretly alive, you could pull the string, which would in turn ring a bell—a sort of Rube Goldberg affair."

"What if no one was around to hear your little bell?" I asked.

John laughed as I worked my jab. It's the introduction, the handshake, the animal sniffing at the new rear end, the establishing punch. The jab is the salesman's calling card. If you can't hit with the jab, you can't hit with anything. Stretch out and present yourself with a firm left, pull back, don't throw wildly. Drive. Don't push.

Had my father always been my jab?

"One, two!" John barked. We moved in circles, and I began to sweat, a new kind of sweat, profound, coming out of my eyes, my feet. I felt dizzy and tried to stabilize by staring at the center of John's face, at a nose that had been broken thirteen times.

John taught me the cross, where you drop your body weight to one side and swing your opposite fist horizontally and hit your opponent, aiming for the face. Sometimes, depending on style and what feels comfortable, you pivot your foot. This can allow more leverage into the blow.

Then my number three punch, the hook. It involves the turning of the core muscles and back, swinging the arm, which is bent at an angle near or at 90 degrees, into your opponent, usually aimed at the side of the head. Later I would learn it for body shots, especially the liver. You can drop a strong man to his knees with a good liver punch. But bodies were almost irrelevant at this stage; it was all about making contact with the punch mitts (also known as "focus pads").

John allowed me brief moments to reconstitute, walk around, and drink some water. My head was swirling with all the information and instructions he'd been giving. I tried to review the punches in my head; I wanted him to think I was a quick study, and maybe that would compensate for any obvious lack of athleticism or conditioning.

Somehow, mercifully, our session ground down to its end. "So that's an hour of boxing," John grinned, assessing my condition while removing my wraps. It occurred to me that this could be the way he weeded people out, in a trial by fire. *Yeah, let's show this nice middle-aged lady what an hour of boxing feels like. She'll get it out of her system.*

"Great! It was just great." My heart was a large orchestral drum and someone was banging on it with enormous mallets. I was practically drooling. What the hell was I thinking?

"You're gonna sleep like a baby tonight," John promised. "Like you just ate a bunch of peanut butter."

I followed him, legs trembling, into his office where I wrote out my first check. My hands shook and I scrawled my name. My signature was straight out of second grade, loopy and insane.

"Don't worry—after a while you'll remember to write out the check first."

I thrilled at his words, trying to mop up some sweat with my shaking hand.

So there would be a next time, a second date?

You'll call me?

John leaned back in his swiveling chair. Then came the diagnosis. *Dry your eyes, doctor's coming in.*

"Well, you have good body mechanics, you're not uncoordinated, and when you relax you have some power. You'll do fine."

I floated on those words for days.

More important, boss was takin' me on.

5

love me, love my cigar

I am six years old and sitting at my father's feet, ducking the flicks of ash from his ever-present and foul-smelling cigar. The large ruby ring on his pinky gleams as he raises his fist. "You bastard!" he yells, leaning forward on his beloved yellow leather club chair with the studded buttons that I fill with chewing gum when he is on the road. "Give 'em hell!" I have no idea who he wants to win, and understand nothing about boxing, but it's Gillette's Friday Night Fights (on the radio it had been the Gillette Cavalcade of Sports), and when the fights are on, the television is his sacred altar and all other activity in our small apartment ceases. My father leaves for his sales trips on Sundays, packing in a gloom, my mother lighting up another Kent and looking on with dread. But on Fridays he returns (when a trip wasn't for two to three weeks at a time), Mommy cooks frozen minute steaks, opens some canned peas, sets the ketchup on the table, and I have a few days to try to figure out what and who the heck this man is who dominates the rhythms of the household and my mother's moods. Watching television together provides most of those opportunities.

Television. A fourteen-year-old Idaho farm boy named Philo T. Farnsworth had a love affair with electricity and it led to the invention of television. In 1928, the *San Francisco Chronicle* described an early set as a "queer looking line image in a bluish light which smudges and blurs frequently." The design had improved by the time my family had one of the few sets on Peshine Avenue in the 1950s, and the image was black and white and absolutely riveting. Children today watching fifty-inch color plasma high-definition screens mounted above fireplaces have no idea how eagerly we huddled around an ugly piece of furniture, turned it on without a remote, waited for it to "warm up," and changed the sparse handful of channels manually, although not without constant negotiations. "You do it! No, you—you're closer!" A test pattern image, often accompanied by the *Star-Spangled Banner*, put the precious baby to sleep. It was called the Indian Head Card and looked like a card from a highly technical Tarot deck, with an Indian in full headdress at the top. To today's agile thumb-texting generation, we may as well have been drawing a box on legs with a set of rabbit ears on the wall of a cave and chanting stories to each other.

"Basilio! Carmen's gonna take him!" Julius chomps down on the stub of his cigar, and I look up at him and redo the rubber bands at the end of my long braids. It's September 23, 1957, and Carmen Basilio is challenging Middleweight Champion of the World Sugar Ray Robinson. It's a match that is famously featured on the cover of *Life* magazine.

I am mystified by my father's love of boxing. He also enjoys watching baseball, particularly the Brooklyn Dodgers, but boxing lights him up like nothing else. My father's own rumored teenage athleticism is like an old trophy—dusty, lost, or buried in a closet under blankets and scrapbooks.

Boxing looks horrible to me—violent, primitive, scary, with few obvious redeeming characteristics. It's a lot like my father, and I don't like him much either. He is a rager, and because his moodiness so frightens me as a child, I can't be very patient or empathetic to his struggles. I certainly don't care that his parents had emigrated from Poland and England, developed a chain of successful bakeries, and then lost everything in the Depression. I don't care that he didn't get to become a journalist because of the Depression, World War II, and the demands of a family. I don't care that he watched Uncle Harry and cousin Joe Klein make millions, donate wings to hospitals, join country clubs, and buy racehorses while Julius toiled on the road, building up the company but never seeing the profits. Instead of having empathy for my father as a tragically unfulfilled man, I see him as childish, selfish, and petulant. I have his number.

In turn, I press his buttons like no one else. They say I was always asking for things—a princess phone, a guitar, my own television. I even once persuaded my parents to buy me a pair of ice skates, although I had never skated and never would. Those size four beauties lay in their box for years. I would run my finger along the blades and tie and untie the laces. The force of my personality incensed my father. He thought he had my number, too, but I wasn't really spoiled; I was desperate. I needed a change, a bright light, a goal, a signal of a shift in the weather pattern of my family's moods and fears.

It is only his hands I see moving—lighting another Corona, working the crossword puzzle, negotiating the oversized plastic steering wheel of a Buick, Rambler, or Oldsmobile (every two years the company leased him a new car) as my sisters and I choke in the back seat, making exaggerated coughing sounds. "Love me, love my cigar!" he'd bellow. I see his hands shaking the dandruff off his scalp. I see his hands removing his socks and shoes in the living room, and scratching his poor dry feet with a vengeance while we winced. "Daddy! Stop!" We begged. "What do you want me to do?" He'd pout.

Or he'd be sitting at a desk at the manufacturing center he called "the Place." "I'm going to the Place this week instead of on the road," he'd say, and I'd be taken along on certain days to the factory in Brooklyn, and select small magnifying glasses, plastic scissors, and miniature dolls out of the enormous barrels in the warehouse, while hair-netted Hispanic workers looked on. Such toys (sold long before the concern about choking hazards) were inserted into "prize boxes," along with taffy that could break your teeth if you just looked at it. In 1953, Harry and Joe Klein purchased a candy business for $25,000. They named it Phoenix Candy and began manufacturing Atlantic-city style saltwater taffy, peanut brittle, and Halloween candy. They only operated seasonally for approximately nine months out of the year, but in 1962 the Kleins had a brainstorm: a more profitable business would come from a confection that they could ship year-round and collect payment within ten days of order, thus ensuring a steady income stream. They brought in vacuum cookers to replace open fire kettles, to save on cooking and boiling time. They bought a new German-made machine—which produced 150 ten-cent bars per minute—and began production of "Now and Later" taffy candy bars. The machine was installed improperly and limped along for about three years until they hired Joseph Stein, a German-speaking plant manager, who fixed it, and the product took off. I remember him.

I was eleven when my father named the taffy "Now and Later" based on the hoarding desire that you could "eat some now, save some for later." He never received any of the profits from its success. This was the family business that put food on our table, but made my father miserable. His sorrow seemed to make my mother fearful and unhappy. She vigilantly scanned his face for keys to his moods. I tried to keep him at a distance.

Still, there was something. Some need for a strong man to lift me up. I'd heard the stories, but it didn't fully compute for me then that my father had been a young man full of potential; handsome, charming, tough. What I saw was that he was overweight, smoked smelly cigars, treated my mother harshly, had an array of medical and dental phobias (as did my mother), and that he seemed completely unable to assert himself with his bosses, who were his relatives. He'd joke about being like Willy Loman in *Death of a Salesman.*

I did like some of his stories, though, especially when they weren't off-color jokes (which embarrassed me to death), and when he recited the long epic poems he knew by heart, like Vachel Lindsay's "The Congo." *Fat black bucks in a wine-barrel room/barrel-house kings with feet unstable.* We understood nothing about the racism in the poem; we just loved the way my father dramatized Lindsay's innovative rhythms. *Boomlay, boomlay, boomlay, Boom.* Ernest Lawrence Thayer's "Casey at the Bat," one of the most famous baseball poems ever written, was a more wholesome tale: *But there is no joy in Mudville—mighty Casey has struck out.*

Julius felt that he himself had struck out, and reminded us of that frequently. He'd wistfully recall a painting he once saw that haunted him. A man is standing over a fence at a racetrack near the paddock where the horses are walked to cool them down. We only glimpse him from the back. His posture is defeated and hulking. At his feet are scattered losing tickets. The title reads "Also Ran." When my sister Susan showed artistic abilities as a young girl, he said, "Paint that for me, won't you? When are you gonna paint the 'Also Ran'? He also often said "Well, I didn't get to write the Great American Novel—now it's up to my daughters." So began the quandary that was to figure throughout my life. Was I supposed to be strong myself? Or find someone else to lean on?

The daughters work to live out the father's dreams?

I hated my father's acrid cigar smoke, yet on every one of my father's birthdays, I walked into Abe's Tobacco Store and asked for "one really really good expensive cigar." "You're a good daughter," Abe would say, smiling at me as he pulled the "Romeo and Juliet" out of the humidor. Each cigar was encased in a long silver tube, a little rocketship to pleasure. *Easy does it, Freudians.* "Good choice," my father would say as he lit up later. I got to keep the case for pencils.

I recently found a photograph taken when I was nine years old. We had accompanied my father on a business trip—this was how we got any family vacations. We spent most of the days at various motels waiting for his return and did our best to have fun without specifically child-centered activities. When my father went off to meet with the brokers, my mother would bring me back a styrofoam container filled with scrambled eggs, bacon, and toast. She let me eat it in bed, and she smoked and watched me while I ate, just like she watched my father eat at the dining room table at home. That lukewarm mess in the container with sections was the most delicious thing I'd ever tasted.

My sister Susan created a photo album with captions written in silver marker: "Websters Motor Court," "Treholm Motor Lodge."

But in one photograph is evidence that we were at some sort of theme park, a Wild Wild West reproduction town in St. Augustine, Florida. I am in shorts and a T-shirt, wearing white anklets and beige loafers. My long thick hair is pulled back into a ponytail. I am awkwardly attempting to sit on the lap of a man in a cowboy hat. I think I can see a faded badge; he's the sheriff maybe. He's sitting on a wooden bench next to a pile of concrete blocks and a grate that simulate an outdoor firepit. He's wearing a thick denim shirt and rugged pants and boots. His eyebrows are bushy and black, like Groucho Marx's, and his eyes are wide open in a startled and fixed way. He smiles past me and never blinks because he is a dummy. I'm straining to try and lean my head on his rigid shoulder, and my right arm is thrown around his neck. My whole body is trying to lean into him, and both my legs are between his.

He is made of god-knows-what, paint is chipping off his ten-gallon hat, and he's just an inert display for the show, but still I'm going for it.

It is a joy to be hidden, but a disaster not to be found.
—D. W. WINNICOTT

I am standing in front of a blue gym mat on the floor of Chancellor Avenue School in Newark, New Jersey. Mr. Kanowith, dense and muscular, is exhaling his onion breath onto me like a dragon digesting its lunch. "Let's go! Are you gonna be a klutz too, like your sister?" I didn't witness her gymnastic travails, but I heard her crying in the bed across from me at night. I knew this humiliation was in her encyclopedia of pubescent hurts, especially since he had called her fat many times. My heart is slamming against my one-piece gymsuit. I tug at its bottom. Everything in grade school happened by height, and I was short, so there was precious little time to prepare. "Form a line!" There I would go, to my place at the front with the other munchkins. *I can do this. I'm not my sister.* I crouch down, trying with all my might to tilt my head and neck backward, tucking them tight like a turtle retreating its head. It is such an unnatural movement I assume I'm going to break in two or faint. Imaginings of discomfort take up residence in my brain and I rehearse them until I am fraught with panic. I clumsily flop over, achieving a semi-roll.

"Klutz!" Mr. Kanowith shouts. "Jerk! Next!" He couldn't use his favorite epithet "Fatso" on me because childhood was my skinny time. I skulk away toward the wooden benches lining the walls where our skirts are folded into small packages and our shoes are neatly tucked, wondering how I can possibly avoid future embarrassment.

I am stealing covetous glances at the agile girls who can do cartwheels, girls who will go on to become popular cheerleaders. They are from another planet, the planet of grace and physical competence. *And, seemingly, no anxiety.*

My friends and I did play hit the penny and stoopball with the pink fuzzless tennis ball called a Spalding on the Newark streets, but it's not the kind of activity that produces sweat. For mysterious reasons, the Spalding sporting goods corporation took the ball off the market in the late 1970s, but I've heard it's being reissued. I'd like to feel one in the palm of my hand again; it holds the memories of games like A—My Name is Alice that involved standing in place, reciting a long alliterative poem while crossing one leg over and under the bounce of the ball in sync with all the letters of the alphabet—a game for a poet, a game for a girl standing still. That was my sport.

"Bombardment!" Mr. Kanowith screams, aroused by his favorite barbaric romp for young girls. Ben Stiller made a silly movie about the game—he called it *Dodgeball.* But because the object of the game was to try to hit, slam, and pound your opponent with a volleyball, anywhere on her body, and became such a brutal ritual, causing even dormant racial tensions to surface, I've always found Bombardment a more fitting name. Newark schools were racially diverse, and the Weequahic section was mainly a mixture of blacks and Jews. In the 1950s and early 1960s, the atmosphere was one of seeming harmony, but kept in balance by lots of segregated table-sitting in the cafeteria. The races gave each other a wide berth. Later on, in my high school years, I watched as the tanks rode up and down the streets during the race rebellion of 1967.

In Mr. Kanowith's class, the black girls take a particular glee in slamming the white girls, and they are better at it. I get hit in the stomach by a tall girl who laughs as she vacuums all the available breath out of me, and I drop to my knees. I try in vain to stand up. From the wall bench, Mr. Kanowith, his arms folded across his chest like an army drill instructor, yells, "Stand up! Walk it off!"

The next gym day I come home at lunchtime and whine, "Mommy, I don't feel good." School is divided into morning and afternoon sessions, and because we live right behind the school, I can come home for lunch and begin my plea.

"If you have a temperature, you can stay home," she'd say, lighting another Kent, which she claimed she never inhaled. Although my mother had a natural intelligence and dreamed of becoming a social worker, after her wartime job testing radio tubes at a factory my father forbade her to work, so she was always home. His daughters could do "anything they set out to do" and would write great books, but his wife must be at home. And there was another reason: my mother was quite agoraphobic. Her own father, Isadore, had died the day after I was born, and that was when she had a breakdown. "She was afraid to hold you," said my eldest sister Mikki, who was twelve when I was born. *So who did hold me?* I wanted to ask. "She was afraid she would drop you." For all my life, I imagined this was her paralyzing anxiety, some desperate feeling of incompetence, but women suffering post-partum depression often want to harm their babies. Imagining anxiety was easier than imagining aggression aimed at me.

No one in those days said "Postpartum depression," and as debilitating and serious as that condition is, the word "breakdown" seemed worse: mysterious, final. Cars and refrigerators broke down. Only people had the hope of enduring.

If only my parents could have had the benefits of Prozac, which was decades away from development. My mother did have Miltown (the Valium of that era), prescribed by Dr. Stern, her psychiatrist. We never knew what Dr. Stern said or did, but I heard that at one point shortly after my birth, electroshock therapy was proposed (as far as I know, the treatment was not carried out but I have no definite proof either way).

While my mother is in the kitchen making me a tuna sandwich, I take the thermometer into the bathroom and run it under hot water. It is a delicate alchemy—too hot and Dr. Flax the gruff doctor might be called; not hot enough, and the perils of gymnastics awaited me. My mom, lonely for her absent husband and happy for my company, lets me stay home, and we begin our unspoken ceremony of avoidance.

We start off sitting on the blue floral couch in the living room to watch *General Hospital.* Then we usually retire to one of the twin beds in my parents' bedroom, where we nap. My mother spends many hours in bed and is always tired. I might awake to the sound of my mother snoring and see by the clock that it is two o'clock. I never question how odd this ritual is. When you're a kid, everything within the house is just all the stuff that happens. At that hour, my classmates would be climbing ropes and hoisting themselves over uneven parallel bars. I try not to think about how much school I am missing, and gently move some part of my body to make contact with hers, perhaps my foot against hers or a hand near her back. I cannot get the feel of my mother. She always seems preoccupied and vacant. I never see her get angry, ever.

Fierce anxiety begins the moment I awake in the morning. I hate presenting my note to the homeroom teacher, always fearing exposure. I dictate the excuse note as my mother writes: "Please excuse Binnie from missing school. She had a sore throat, stomachache, headache, 24-hour virus (we rotated the causes to avoid suspicion), and I thought it best to keep her home." By then I pretty much *have* a headache or stomachache—from the guilt and lies alone.

"I thought it best to keep her home." That is my mother's original contribution, restrained but elegant, and that exact phrase ends every note.

I have a photograph, a companion piece to the one of me at the Wild Wild West theme park. My mother is sitting in a rocking chair on a long porch. I assume it is one of the rooming houses we stayed at in Saratoga Springs, New York. Because my father loved the track, he'd combine a business trip to a broker in Albany with a long stop in Saratoga, the elegant and old-fashioned racetrack where a gregarious black woman named "Chicken Sadie" sold fried chicken and lemonade. When I didn't go along to the track, I sat on the front porch swatting flies and drinking bottled Cokes out of a giant cooler, like a kid in a Truman Capote short story.

In this photograph, I am younger than in the Wild West picture, maybe six years old. Like many kids, I had a doctor's kit. I'm wearing a stethoscope around my neck, and, head cocked, I'm looking intently at my mother, who is obligingly allowing me to take her temperature. I'm sure she'd have wanted to stay home, too, pretty much all the time, with that slight fever that enabled avoidance but didn't summon the authorities. I look like I'm trying hard to figure out exactly what is wrong with her, and it's the most difficult case of my short career.

After too many excuse notes stack up, the truant officer appears at our house. That's what happened in those days. He presents my mother with a written record of all the days I have missed, pointing out that they are all gym days. The jig is up on my life of crime. I'm trapped. Mr. Kanowith hovers around the corner like a crazy dog you must pass on the way to school, and there's no other way to go.

There was nothing left to do but tell my father. My sisters and I winced through the countless times when he would erupt at the dining room table because the meat was too tough, yelling and storming out, or become angry at our mother for something we didn't understand. Once, during a Saturday matinee at the Rialto Theatre, where they played a newsreel, cartoons, and two features for twenty-five cents, we were watching *Elmer Gantry* starring Burt Lancaster as a volatile and corrupt evangelist. Suddenly my father rose from his seat and stormed down the aisle to lift a noisy teenage boy by the collar. "Shut up!" my father yelled, while the audience yelled "Go, Elmer, Go!" and we cringed down further in our seats.

Maybe with the gym teacher my father's rage could at last be useful.

My sister and I tittered with a giddy delight. It was thrilling and nauseating, the prospect of Daddy confronting the gym teacher. We never found out exactly what was said or done, but we were never expected to do backward somersaults again.

Mr. Kanowith continued to teach girls' gym.

When my father wasn't on the road selling candy, he drove us everywhere—to the Pic 'N Pay supermarket, Ming's Chinese restaurant, Kartzman's delicatessen, and Halem's candy store where I sipped egg creams and bought *Superman* and *Modern Romance* comics. Occasionally my girlfriends and I, experimenting with teased hair and absurdly tight pants, trekked from one schoolyard to another in hot pursuit of boys. I suppose you could consider that exercise. But mostly, the joys of the physical world were almost completely foreign, and bodies were more often a source of shame and pain. I watched my mother take to her bed with frequent migraine headaches, especially on Sundays when my father would visit his ex-wife and their son, my half-brother, who lived in Brooklyn with his mother, Rose. We rarely saw them. My brother Gary's entire existence was shrouded in confusion. *He's not your whole brother,* we would hear from my mother—*it's not the same mother*. But she was reluctant to explain much more. I asked my sisters over and over: "So is he our stepbrother?" Was he less related because it wasn't the same mother rather than the same father? It strained my brain the way algebra did, and I wasn't the only one in the house suffering cognitive dissonance over this. *Everyone* looked dazed when the topic came up.

I never knew why my parents didn't swim. My father had been in the Navy—I guess World War II occasioned a significant lapse in standards of acquatic proficiency. Lakes, oceans, rivers, and all deep waters were mostly appreciated on postcards. Our trips to Atlantic City or Coney Island were mainly for Nathan's hot dogs and arcade games. But I was still drawn to the water. If only I could find someone not phobic, maybe I could learn. I persuaded my parents to send me to Camp Nageewa. I really wanted to escape the claustrophobia of our small apartment and was breaking new ground; neither of my older sisters had been to sleepaway camp. It was a fresh start. As my parents drove me through the wilds of the Garden State Parkway to deposit me at camp, I felt my life opening up. Across the lake was a boys' camp, and we had dances with those boys, whose sweaty hands gripped ours to the sounds of "Earth Angel." The girls wore their best mohair sweaters. On Friday nights I wore a white "skort"—the latest fad—a combination of a shorts and a skirt, and sang some Hebrew songs, which were strange and exotic to me.

At camp I adapted fairly well to the crafts activities, the games, mealtime, and friendships with the girls in my cabin. But the first day of assessment of our swimming skills at the lake was a fearsome confrontation with my secret. I accurately identified myself as a beginner, a "tadpole," while other girls zoomed past into advanced sections. Inauspicious beginnings—the swimming counselor decided not to learn my name. When I first repeated it to her, she looked blank and then annoyed, as if it were a mathematical equation she knew she'd never master. "That's too hard; I'll never remember it," she said casually. "I'll call you B." So she gave up on my name altogether and, almost simultaneously, we both gave up on my learning to swim.

I'm not proud to admit I hid out through the lessons in the shallowest part of the lake, doing a clumsy dog paddle and scraping my knees along the bottom of the lake. It's not like I didn't try; it's just that I was falling through the cracks, or waves, as the counselor and everyone else ignored me. One day there was a contest to see who could hold their head underwater the longest. I watched mutely as the other little girls dunked and popped back up. I couldn't imagine it, water getting in my eyes, ears, nose, and mouth! It seemed horrible and frightening. So I just stood stock-still and waited in agony for the contest to be over, praying I would not be noticed.

As with my partially successful truancy on gym days, I discovered a loophole to help me avoid the now daily horror of swimming. If you had your period, you could go out in a rowboat instead of swim. I loved the rowboat. Safe in my lifejacket, I ate baloney sandwiches and drank grape Kool-Aid. One day, after saying I had my period for perhaps the fifth consecutive day, the counselor narrowed her eyes and said, "Again? Or *still*?" Her words chill me to this day. *Again? Or still!* It was like those dreams where you appear naked in front of an auditorium of people, or a front tooth keeps falling out, or you've forgotten where your next class is. I don't know what I answered, but pretty soon after that, my parents arrived for Visiting Day. I sobbed over the bucket of fried chicken they brought, confessed my swimming dilemma, and my father had another one of his "talks" with the swimming counselor who had shamed me, probably something along the lines of "leave my daughter alone, damn it!" "*She stays where she is!*" he had yelled to the limo of gangsters, clutching his beloved Alice. From then on, there was no pressure on me to swim. The relief was enormous, but carried a frisson of guilt and shame.

When I arrived home after camp I was eager for Coca-Cola and the familiar comforts. Heading toward the television, I noticed with alarm that the birdcage was gone. Our parakeet Nicky had died while I was away and my parents had decided not to tell me. "We wanted to protect you," they protested while I wept.

Backward somersaults, dental visits, swimming, bird deaths, truths about previous marriages and divorce, information about Gary—it was all deemed "too much" and wrapped up under the dark cloak. When I was eighteen, my middle sister Susan sat me down in a coffee shop and confided conspiratorily: "Daddy married Rose first, and they had Gary. Meanwhile Mommy was married to another man." *Married? Mommy was married before? How can that be?* It was as if she was born only when she met my father.

"That's not all," she said. "Mommy and Daddy met and fell in love, but guess who Mommy was married to?" I cringed. "Rose's brother Willie!"

This news made me nauseous; the sheer shock of it. So they were both still married—to a brother and sister pair—when they fell in love and it was a huge scandal in Brooklyn. That's why they fled to New Jersey. They were actually living together. Now *that* was a *shanda*. I learned later that Mikki, my eldest sister, had to be officially adopted by Daddy because she had Willie Wilensky's name, Mommy's first husband.

I need to go back to school . . . *grade school*. Who could understand these complex computations, shrouded as they were with enormous emotion, shame, and fear? If only I could start over with more of the actual *facts*.

Not having any kind of athletic life as a child, I continued to excel at reading, writing, and doing imitations of Joan Crawford and Bette Davis, my strong female role models who prevailed through their wits and their haughty self-righteousness. I tried to ignore their small waists. My mother and sisters were inching up toward more Slavic silhouettes every day, and I suspected that was my future, too.

Still, a longing remained. I could not give up on the fantasy of being more like the active girls. I peered through the slats of the venetian blinds in our den, with its view of the playground next door, and watched mournfully as the popular girls played softball. I wanted to run fast, hit hard, and wear a cute uniform. These girls seemed to know something about life I didn't. I wanted to move comfortably through space without feeling unsteady. Later, in high school, I read Simone de Beauvoir's journals, in which she described having a body so strong and hungry for exercise she could barely satisfy it. She took monstrous hikes, packing a tidy little bag of plums as her sensuous reward that she savored on a picturesque bench in the French countryside.

When we accompanied my father on his trips, I begged from the backseat for a motel with a pool, as if there in some godforsaken place in Ohio or Pennsylvania I would find my sea legs and start swimming when no one was watching. By then my eldest sister was off at New York University studying clinical psychology. My middle sister was profoundly disinterested in pools (she later became a philosopher who challenged Descartes' notion that the mind and body are separate). So I took on the strange and lonely vigil, like Linus watching his beloved blanket spin round and round in the washing machine, just out of reach. Late at night, having driven for endless hours in this futile quest, my father chomped his cigar with renewed sullenness. "Look, there's a Vacancy sign at that motel," he'd say. "But Daddy, there's no pool!" I'd whine, as if I couldn't miss a single day of training.

My father, perhaps out of guilt over his long absences, colluded in the illusion that a pool was necessary for our nonswimming family. He drove on, searching for yet another motel, despair and fatigue building in the car. Once the motel with pool was secured, I'd usually go in but once during our entire stay, get wet, flap around in the shallow end or float in an inner tube, shriek and giggle with happiness, and thank my parents. I have the photographs to prove it.

Please, please, let there be a pool!

Cushioned by my parents' own fears, protected from challenges by my father's rages (and in some ways, can you blame him—gym teachers and swimming counselors like the ones we endured would never be tolerated in today's child-sensitive world), encouraged by my teachers to cultivate my intellect, I didn't feel terribly aware of my body or its positive potential.

My eldest sister finally learned to swim at fifty years old. "See?" She marveled as I watched her breaststroke through a pool. "See how buoyant we are?" I was awestruck and proud, but I knew that by "we" she didn't mean humans, she meant *us*, we three sisters, and probably our relatives, and only reinforced my notion that our bodies were too fat for this world and that we belonged to a small sect of unsinkable Slavic women with heavy thighs.

Many, many years later, when I did find my own body's strength, began to box, and study the lives of champions, I read

Muhammad Ali's poem about the categories of the heart—the heart of iron that is changed though the fire, the heart of gold that needs the sun's glory to achieve its image, and the "craven heart of wax" that "melts before heat." But then there is "the heart of paper that flies like a kite in the wind. One can control the heart of paper as long as the string is strong enough to hold it. But when there is no wind, it drops."

Inside the bell jar of our small Newark apartment, I had no wind at my back to force my body to move.

Multiple decades later, the weather pattern finally changed, and while my father had repeatedly taken me out of the ring, John kept pushing me back in, and I got this chance because I fell in my own backyard.

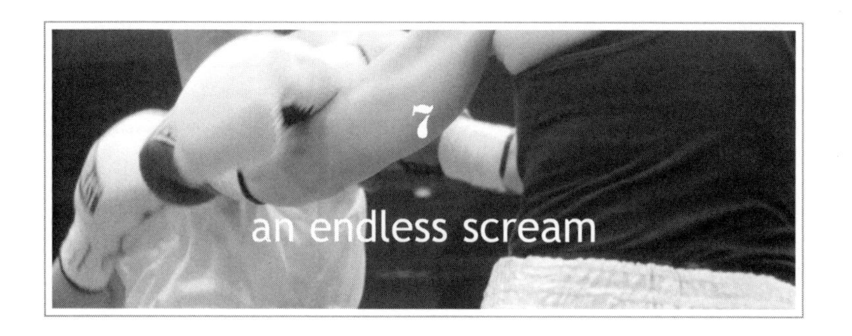

7
an endless scream

I felt like an endless scream through nature.
—EDVARD MUNCH

Before John there was Jacob, like a bible story. I met him when I broke my ankle and foot, and that's one of the injuries I didn't tell John about in my zeal to be seen as a strong and worthy disciple of boxing.

Several years before John took me on, there was a morning when I was distracted and spacey as I carried a can of birdseed through the house, out onto the deck. I was on my way to the feeder in the backyard when suddenly, the hand of Hermes reached out from the underworld and grabbed my sandaled foot, drawing me down where I was yanked across the grass, landing on all parts of my body; it was as if I had no hands to use whatsoever. My yell was unearthly—metal shards clanging, the ferocious AAAARRRGGHHH! of cartoon spills.

This was the real beginning of the boxing. You might say I fell into it. It was a Saturday morning, and I was alone in the house except for Griffin and Sabine, our small Havanese dogs; my husband, Scott, had gone to help with weekend inventory at the wine distributor where he worked. Around the time of the accident in my backyard, I was becoming that most embarrassing of things, a middle-aged woman wishing she were young again. It helped that my husband was ten years younger, and I was happy to inform anyone who was interested that that was the case. Producing a music program at an alternative radio station also helped me feel young, and in fact, that's where I met Scott. He and his creative partner Ken had completed a series of fundraising spots for WPKN spoofing *Twin Peaks*, and these impressive pieces, full of sound effects and original music, led to Scott securing a regular time slot, "Leaving the Twentieth Century with No Regrets," a contemporary classical music program. My show, "A Miniature World," was a sound collage of indie rock, electronica, quirky stuff, along with readings, interviews, and a feature about my interest in primates.

We live and work near a university town, which brings an odd mixture of cultural benefits and sorrows. There are great lectures by esteemed professors, sophisticated bookstores, good concerts, but I am always surrounded by the young and optimistic, and this leads to a really bad habit—working the rough and familiar touchstone of my envy, its edges filled with students' futures, their freshness and advantages.

I'm not an inactive therapist—I talk, I engage, I laugh—but there is an aspect to this psychic midwifery, delivering people up to themselves, that can sometimes make me feel like I'm disappearing. There was one day when I glanced up to check my reflection in the window of a small coffee shop, and there was nothing there. Something about the angle, maybe, but still I thought, I am truly invisible now. Wasn't it vampires who cast no reflection?

Another problem—I was in a period of romanticizing my wild teenage years. I had a black-and-white image in mind of myself at age sixteen. It's also from a photograph. I am standing in black jeans and a sleeveless black top, locket around my neck, my long hair parted in the middle. I am wearing loafers without socks and leaning against a tree, a cigarette dangling from what I hoped was a wise and knowing smile. Around my neck is a large, boxy camera on a long leather strap that had I borrowed from my first boyfriend, who had gone off to Goddard College in Vermont. It is his picture that is inside the locket. A few months later he joined the Weathermen, the radical activist group of the 1960s, along with several of my friends. Every event of those days was full of meaning and intensity, with a gravitas to rival any Shakespearean play (we thought). Many years later, in one of those Google-facilitated reunions, my young love told me that the Weathermen experience was a huge disappointment. They separated couples, took away books and belongings, and forced everyone to take psychedelic drugs and have group sex in an attempt to raise consciousness. No kidding. He was asked to throw rocks at a police station. He had to call his father to come and pick him up from one of the collectives, sneaking out in the dead of night.

Whatever the realities of the past were, I still needed to deal with aging, so I developed a game. Away from mirrors, I pretended that I looked somehow the same as when I was young, at least from the neck up. I tried to feel like my eyes looked out of that younger self by accessing some spirit or essence of that being and pushing it forward, as if I were exhaling it. The game worked best when I was with someone my own age or older. I could focus on the signs of their aging, whether it be a heavily lined neck, or greying hair, and feel . . . pity. My day would come, but back then I was in that nether region, being shepherded across the River Styx, not young, but not old. We read the obituaries to measure our time left. Died at eighty? Ninety? Good. That's far off.

My all-too-desperate plea to my hair stylist every few months also became "oh my god please don't make me look conservative!" It had become a phobia. Gel helps, a balm against the shocking utterances of gas station boys and store clerks who no longer call you "Miss." The slide from "Miss" to "Ma'am" happens gradually, like watching your dog age. You don't notice all at once the increasing droop of the jowls, the dotting of white in the fur, the hesitation at doorways, or the occasional melancholy stare, as if remembering a carefree jog through a field. It all proceeds in tiny increments. One day your sweet pup is fourteen, and you are mopping up accidents and patting his head with the tender feeling of rehearsing how to let go. "Ma'am" urged me further into static waters, having waded in unknowingly, to join the aunts, grandmothers, and other desexed entities.

I wanted to scream out: "Hey, don't you see my leather jacket, my perky step, my impertinent grin?" But it was a defense. I did not feel vital and alive. I did not feel connected to any real community. Without children, the map of where to go and what to do next was a bit more fuzzy and indistinct. My parents were gone, and for reasons I didn't completely understand, my sisters and I were estranged from any extended family. It was as if *everyone* had died. We had no contact with my mother's sisters and brothers, nor with my father's side of the family.

The day of the accident I had awoken in a distraught state from one of my recurrent dreams about tiny babies. Maybe these babies were the "might-have-beens." Yet the prospect of being a mother myself had always seemed remote. Motherhood was dangerous; it could send you down a long dark well where you could lose your identity and become dependent on others' rescue. I told myself that I didn't want to pass on my genes. A kind social worker tried to convince me that was tragic. "Look at all the people having children. They don't think twice about what they're passing on!" But I was unconvinced. When I'm feeling more at peace with being childless/childfree, I say things like: It's because parenting requires you to have a unified theory of being human (which maybe I was supposed to have by being a therapist), which I never had. Or maybe children force you to create one. Either way, I was not sucking the juice out of life, pumping up paltry rituals like Halloween, and explaining everything I knew about manners and geography to a small being in a public place. But I can hear the bitterness.

When I felt pure grief was when the dreams occurred—babies that I rescued from danger, tenderly held, and understood completely and effortlessly. In waking life, though, I had terrible problems with the sound of children crying, especially as I walked through supermarkets, not the most gentle of terrains for parents, who are understandably stressed and sometimes impatient with their toddlers. To me it sounded like all children were in agony and that their parents were unresponsive. Knowing that it was probably triggered by memories of my mother's postpartum depression did not change the way the sounds reached me.

Meanwhile, back on the ground, clutching at the earth, I felt an abstract and disembodied ripping in my leg. Sweat began its determined creep across my body. Had it been just the day before, my cries would have disrupted the rhythmic chatter of the Portuguese workmen trimming the pear trees on the neighboring farm. De de de de DA DA—they would have dropped their pointy-topped orchard ladders, climbed the hill, and lifted me with strong arms. I wouldn't have cared about my bare hairy legs splayed out, I would have wanted only rescue. But on Saturdays the men stayed home and cleaned their cramped barracks.

My god, why was I on the ground? I groped around and found what had done me in. It was not even a proper hole, just a deep indentation with some loosened clumps of grass now scattered around. I squeezed the grass and dropped it back into the depression, as if fixing the earth was a job I could accomplish as a fallen body. A deep primal instinct commanded me to move. I crawled to the house through the deep brush onto my deck, like a combat soldier, flailed out toward the railing, hoisting myself, but keeping my body low to keep from passing out. Through a series of crawls, hops, and wall-grabbing that haunted me in days to come like an intrusive stuck song fragment, I made it to the kitchen where I slid to the floor beside the refrigerator. That was deliberate; I knew I needed ice. The freezer being on the bottom had seemed so odd when we bought the house, and now I was grateful for it. I pulled out a frozen bag of edamame soybeans, slapped it on my ankle, and wondered what would happen if I did indeed faint. I don't know how, but I managed to grab the telephone.

Scott wasn't easily reachable in the recesses of the wine warehouse, so I called my sister Susan, who was living and teaching in

Kentucky. We had soothed each other through many a medical mystery, too often preferring our own homespun advice to immediate medical attention. Susan diagnosed a sprained ankle, and ordered ice and Advil. But Advil was way up high in the smoky mountains of the kitchen cabinetry, requiring a trek for which I was woefully unprepared. I slid the frozen vegetables around on my ankle and let my sister's voice keep me from slipping into unconsciousness. "I've had this happen," she said. Whatever I go through, it has happened to her—loss of vision from a migraine, GI symptoms, dizziness, stuffed ears, rashes, intractable urinary infections.

I eyed the cabinets. If men in war could drag themselves through horrific terrains on wounded legs to get to safety, to help each other, I could get to a bottle of pills in a kitchen cabinet. I tucked the frozen bag into my shirt pocket. Then I crawled to the couch in the living room and hoisted myself up, inserted pillows under my leg, and repositioned the iced beans.

Every few minutes, my ankle and foot throbbed in new places, little knives and forks sawing away at them; Advil could only do so much. No one was coming; it was just me and my ungraceful body. *That necessary backpack.*

A gust of leaves slapped against the sliding door to the deck, reminding me of how breezy it had felt before I fell, like a storm was coming.

The pain was getting worse, not better.

Luckily, Scott checked in from work and hurried home. We continued Dr. Susie's treatment plan, but by the next morning, the pain was extreme.

In weeks to come I experienced the diagnosis ("I hope you have a good orthopedist," droned the ER physician) of a broken ankle and a broken foot, horrible pain, and immobilization from a cast for eight weeks. I worked on some writing, Scott brought in take-out sushi and helped me shower with a trash bag over my cast, held in place with a rubber band. I looked like a homeless person warding off the cold and the wet. I had a few long, rambling telephone conversations with long-distance friends, lubricated by pain meds and diminished responsibilities. Truth be told, I loved not going to work. I felt tender toward my immobilized state, taking my time at the bathroom sink, savoring the small tasks I could accomplish, like wiping the faucets clean with tiny repetitions and organizing my jewelry. I slept deeply, on my back, mouth open, the sleep of vacations and long naps. I marveled at my ability to sleep despite the awkwardness of the heavy cast. If I chose not to dress, to spend the day in mismatched pajamas, who could judge? I drifted through my days pulled only by my own desires, reading, writing, watching television. My little dogs Griffin and Sabine peered up at me from their post down at my ankle, where their heads lay across the cast; it must have felt cool and sturdy under their chins, like a porcelain tube.

"Don't forget to fill in the hole in the yard," I said to Scott from my bed.

"I will, I will."

I had no life experiences to reassure me that broken bones really healed, but of course I survived this, my first broken bone of my entire life. There was no tale to tell later of an exotic skiing accident or rock-climbing incident. When Suszannah Warner, a young boxing champion from England, discovered boxing it was also because of an injury; she severely tore the infamous anterior cruciate ligament during a soccer game, and during rehab she wanted to find a sport that was easier on the knees. She chose boxing. My leg had simply descended into an animal hole and snapped.

Actually, I do carry the scar of two stitches in my chin. When I was nine years old, one Yom Kippur, Dr. Flax, the gruff doctor who made a house call if I overshot the mark on the thermometer during truant gym days and tended our typical array of childhood diseases (German measles, mumps, chicken pox), was aggravated because he had been called by my parents on that highest of holy days. He had been on his way to synagogue.

"No stitches, right?" I begged, holding a bloody washcloth under my chin, watching the drops hit the leather seat in the back of the Oldsmobile and squeezing my eldest sister's hand. She was home from college for a visit. Other kids with injuries and stitches we'd seen were the veterans of foreign wars, while we'd been exempt from service.

"Of course no stitches," my parents assured me as if their lives depended on it, "that gaping hole in your chin simply needs a special band-aid, one that Dr. Flax will have in his office." In those days, lying to children was common and useful in such moments. My eldest sister was once gaily dressed, told she was going to a birthday party, and diverted to the hospital to have her tonsils removed. Hospital attendants actually had to hold her down while she screamed in the elevator.

That night, despite my orthodox grandmother's exhortations at me in Yiddish (by then we had moved her from Brooklyn to a small attic apartment above the two-family we were renting) to not ride my bicycle, I ignored her shaking head and her universal language of warning. That was *mein bubehs deigeh* (my grandmother's worry). Yom Kippur, after all, is the highest of holy days, a day of atonement and prayer, but that observance was for others, and I stubbornly wanted to get away from that Old World fear. Years ago a friend gave me a funny pin that read: "What fresh hell is this?" That must have been how my grandmother felt, watching us kids prance around in this new country. *Voos far a meshigas iz doos?* (what sort of madness is this?) would be her cry. Bicycle riding got me out of the house, and was my only exercise, albeit quite a slow and distracted one, as I rode Peshine Avenue and Bergen Street as if they were gently paved lanes alongside an ocean. This Sunday night, however, I was heading down a hill experimentally, and the front tire caught on a discarded bobby pin, probably one that had hoisted a teased hairdo. I tumbled over the handlebars, and hit the concrete. *Grandma was right—here's the punishment.* My chin split open, and by the amount of gushing blood you would have predicted a trip to the emergency room, except I wailed "No hospital!" to my frightened parents, as if I'd had traumatic experiences in hospitals across the world, and that's why Dr. Flax was late to shul that Yom Kippur. They may as well have called the gym teacher to examine me—they were quite similar in their impatience and mishandling of children. Dr. Flax had a smashed-in nose, too, like my sadistic gym teacher. I was being bullied in my formative years by a legion of George C. Scott clones.

Dr. Flax grumbled as he let us into the office, and proceeded to carve two stitches into my chin without benefit of anesthetic. I tried not to scream. My parents fretted in the waiting room, while my tonsilless sister stood by and gripped my hand. Afterward, Dr. Flax suffered an attack of kindness and announced with admiration that I had the strength of ten men. Or was it courage? Maybe, despite my many fears, I had even a small dose of that mystical quality that the boxing community calls *heart*. At least I hoped so.

There was another authoritative and sadistic male figure in my childhood—the dentist. Although Dr. Craig handed out small charms from a jar on his desk (I particularly coveted a tiny bathtub and a plastic hot dog, complete with roll), he was strict and impatient. Was this so long ago they didn't have novocaine? Or did he just withhold it? I squirmed as he drilled.

"No nonsense, Binnie, no nonsense," he warned.

I cried when the nurse removed my leg cast and I saw my forlorn foot, still a bit swollen. It looked foreign and vulnerable, the skin flaking and the toes huddling together.

"Ya want me to put it back on? Wipe your eyes, doctor's coming in," she barked, practically throwing a tissue at me. This orthopedic practice got low points for bedside manner. The doctor was a former football player who'd gone to medical school and made no eye contact. Still longing for the rapport that had evaded me with all healthcare providers of my childhood, I asked him at my first visit if he missed playing sports. "Ah, those were the days," he said wistfully, and insisted that my taking Oxycodone was ridiculous. "This pain is nothing," he said, looking across the room at a skeletal chart, obviously recalling blood, sweat, and tearing ligaments on the field.

And so I graduated to an air cast, which I could remove at night, and soon it was time for physical therapy sessions, exercises with long colorful rubber bands, hot and cold treatments, and ultimately, at my request, aquatherapy. *Please let there be a pool at the next motel.* I just couldn't give it up.

In the warm water pool at the Gaylord Rehabilitation Center, where Christopher Reeves sometimes received treatment (on those nights the pool was closed to the rest of us), I felt strong and almost athletic. All around me the elderly and disabled, their varicose veins like pieces of a dark and foreboding sky, commenced their glacial stroll through the water, and, at least once an hour, someone in a wheelchair would be deposited into the water hydraulically, in an orange plastic seat, the kind found in old cafeterias, attached to a crane. Most wheelchair inhabitants I saw at the Rehab Center had a pasty pallor. Often their feet were pink and swollen, or turned and facing one direction, sad and resigned, like leftovers. Tenderly the attendants would lower them in, then hose them off in a mystical ritual at the end. Some had been in accidents, some had strokes, some had congenital problems.

In this crowd I was an Olympian.

After physical therapy had helped my ankle and foot considerably, I went to my local gym where I hoped to find a personal trainer who could help me gain even more strength and confidence. I would try to make my ankle stronger than ever before . . . I would not go gently into that good night.

The pictures on the wall of the local Bally's gym were filled with images of eager but distressingly young certificate-bearers offering their personal trainer services. "Jacob" caught my eye—I'd seen his joyous smile, and he'd had experience with the elderly (a detail becoming more and more appealing), according to his bio. He was a few credits shy of becoming a physical therapist. Of all the possibilities, he seemed less likely to flaunt annoying slogans of "no pain, no gain," and more equipped than most to administer CPR, which was comforting.

Our first six months were less than memorable. Patiently, he led me through balance exercises, sat me on a giant ball, taught me proper sit-ups, and tried to keep me moving. We called my broken ankle "the bad one" and tenderly stretched it. Jacob was a devout Catholic who asked me one day if I believed in God. I thought of Julian Barnes' line "I don't believe in God, but I miss him," from his memoir, *Nothing to be Frightened Of.* Instead I said, "I don't know. I wish I did know something." From then on, our sessions were peppered with intimate discussions about the mysteries of the universe while jocks paraded by and young women sipped vitamin-enhanced water through plastic straws.

Jacob was a lovely antidote to my grade-school gym teacher/tyrant. He was kind, supportive, and nonjudgmental. Still, I never looked forward to going to the gym until one day I noticed a wire basket of boxing gloves and punching mitts. It was then that I picked up a weird stone and asked Jacob if we could box. Jacob glowed with enthusiasm. "You want me to teach you to box? I think I can do that—I took a workshop."

He sorted through the wire box and decided on a pair of twelve-ounce black gloves for me, helped me put my hands inside, and strapped the Velcro tight at the wrists. The first thing you notice about boxing gloves is how heavy they are.

The exhilaration from boxing was immediate. I sweated more, and moved more than I had in ages. If Jacob was late, I'd grab the gloves and punch mitts and stake out some territory for us in the middle of the gym. Gradually the sit-ups, balancing, and weight lifting faded, and all we did was box. I began to look forward to our sessions at the gym. In the following months, my bad leg got stronger. I still worried about it and wondered if the stiffness would ever completely go away. We even did some kickboxing. Jacob held a padded shield in front of him, and I strode forward, knocking him backward as I kicked out. "Heeya!" I'd shout, as if herding cattle on an episode of *Bonanza.* He taught me to roundhouse kick. Side by side, we crouched in deep squats, with Jacob holding a smaller shield, and I would whip around and slam the shield with my outer leg. My body surprised me—it assumed unfamiliar positions eagerly, as if it were agile and strong. This began my experience of my body as having a double life. There was the sturdy, eager, and uncomplaining body of the training, and the after-hours body, with its plump, fleshy passivity and its mundane aches and pains.

I occasionally saw a few other, much younger women in the gym who put on gloves and hit their trainer's punch mitts, but it was still enough of an unexpected sight to see a woman punching that other trainers began to acknowledge me with respectful nods. One day an older guy wearing a wide leather back support belt watched me punching for a while, and said, "Whoa! I wouldn't want to get her mad at me!"

After a few months, Jacob declared that he had taken me as far as he could go, that what I enjoyed most in exercise was feeling my strength, and that maybe I needed a real boxing coach. A *coach*? I was someone who couldn't always hold onto the outlines of my own body. What would I do with a coach?

After I'd been boxing for a few months, my husband Scott began to ask questions.

"Uh—where is this all going to go?"

"What do you mean?" I asked innocently.

"Well, you know, I know it's great exercise, but just how far are you going with it? Do you want to be in the ring?"

I couldn't answer. Just how far did I want to go? Or, perhaps more important, at my advanced age, how far *could* I go?

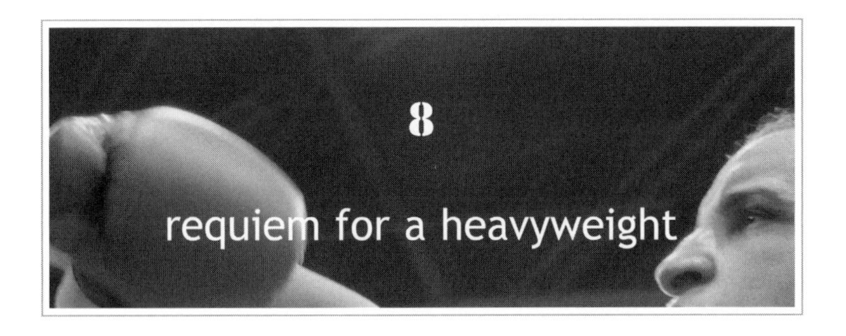

8

requiem for a heavyweight

Before John took me on, and during the months that Jacob and I were boxing at the gym, my husband was going through a personal dry spell. He was obsessed with a table-top baseball game with cards and dice in which you could reproduce the teams of a certain game in a certain year but be the pretend manager, so you could make everything come out differently. When he wasn't doing this he was watching reruns of old Red Sox games.

When Scott spoke of his childhood, I pictured a Norman Rockwell painting, in which he was a little towheaded boy whose hair was being ruffled by his sisters, as Mom called everyone in for Jell-o with fruit floating in it.

Whereas my family was hugging the furniture, balancing food on our laps, and kibbitzing, Scott's white Anglo-Saxon Protestant family was swimming, playing tennis and ping-pong. While my dad sat molded to his club chair, enjoying the fights on television, Scott's dad was out mowing the lawn, restoring an antique automobile, or building a gazebo. Scott's younger sister received a full tennis scholarship to the University of Hartford, which she accepted. In his early years in Sudbury, Massachusetts, Scott enjoyed a veritable sports arena in his own backyard, where the ground sloped down to a huge flat playing surface where neighborhood kids gathered throughout the seasons for baseball, football, and soccer. A short trip one street away led to a pond where they caught bullfrogs in the summer and ice-skated in the winter. Scott played Little League baseball. The family moved to New Hartford, New York, when he was in fifth grade, and Scott played there, then moved to Trumbull, Connecticut, where his Dad coached many of the teams. Scott drew the nickname "Hero" in Frisbee football games because of the long passes he would catch.

Of course, all of this glorious physicality eventually petered out, and in a recent attempt to reignite his baseball career, Scott joined his company's softball team. I was excessively excited, even considered starting a cheerleading squad. We could both redo our childhoods. We shopped together for his baseball pants and cleats. But it was hardly a return to glory. When he arrived at the field, he discovered his baseball pants were a size too small, and the white socks he had grabbed in the dim light of the early morning turned out to be pink. (I had laundered them mixed together with a red sweater.) He survived the chuckles from teammates and onlookers, and got a hit when he was up at bat. It rolled to the outfield, and on his merry way to first base he pulled his hamstring. I'd never seen a bigger bruise; it was like a large slice of burnt toast on the back of his leg. After sitting out a few games, like a trooper he rejoined the team, only to pull the hamstring on his opposite leg, and that was that.

One night I came home from the gym, all proud and pumped from my own workout, and the sight of Scott's Honda sitting in the garage made me crazy, because he'd planned to go out to hear a local band and obviously hadn't gone. I was over-invested in this outing because lately he was spending so much time at home. I could see the fun of following a sports team like the Red Sox, the perpetual underdogs, and the satisfaction in having such control in the baseball board game, but we both tended to be a bit isolative. A few years prior, busting out of another creative vacuum, Scott worked up a stand-up comedy routine and performed with the New England Acting Theatre at a local coffeehouse. He was a smash hit—I've got the laughs on tape. Scott had a huge talent for telling stories, being funny. Everyone was always encouraging him to do more comedy, but he wasn't great with following up.

I didn't go into the house; instead I drove to the parking area at the fire station down the street. One thing I had learned from being married for many years was that sometimes you had to protect your spouse from yourself. My technique was to call ahead. "Just wanted to warn you—I had an awful day and I'm feeling insane; please don't take it personally." Thank god for cellphones.

This time I hadn't really had an awful day, but the sight of his car, all passively tucked away, was a harbinger of a long winter of replayed baseball games.

I dialed and barely squeaked out a hello.

"Hi, honey." He was sweet and always calling me honey.

My silence built into its pit of despair.

"Why are you home?" I spit out the question.

"What do you mean, that I didn't go to the concert?"

"Yes. Exactly. You said you were going."

"I just felt kinda . . . tired."

The coils of data that wind around couples and family utterances are dense and refer back to other conversations, other people, disappointments, fears, every word and gesture packed with meaning. A conversation that might sound benign to an eavesdropper holds all the portent and shading of a Harold Pinter play, as if we carry the secrets of each others' crimes, jealously guarded against the outside world but ready at a moment's notice to be pulled out of our bag of tricks for vengeance.

"What's going on? We talked about this! You've been in all week, doing baseball."

"It relaxes me . . ."

"Yeah, but you're going to relax into a stupor. I mean, at least I have the boxing. I mean we have to have things to bring each other, into the relationship," (an insufferably modern concept). "I'm worried about you."

And so it went. He defended, I attacked, I softened, he meandered.

The weekend was tense. I did a lot of compulsive cleaning, and he played guitar in his study. We circled each other. It became less and less clear what the fight, if you could call it that, was really about.

One night he said, "I'm going to an improvisation workshop down at Yale."

My heart swelled. Things were moving again.

A few nights later: "I'm auditioning at a local community theater."

Wow. Things were moving fast. "Oh? What's the play?"

"*Requiem for a Heavyweight.*"

"Wow. That's a great play. I saw it as a kid. What would be your part? Oh my god! And it's about boxing!" One of *the* saddest stories I'd ever seen, in *Requiem* the aging boxer protagonist meets the utmost disgrace at the end of his career, as he is made into a tomahawk-wielding, costumed joke. The film always made me cry, and the boxer's unhappiness and defeat, although extreme, well, you can probably guess who they reminded me of. It's also a story about those beckoning arms of corruption—the boxer's manager owes money to the mob, so he's expected to get his fighter to take a dive. The Faustian dilemma.

"I don't know—I got hold of the script at the library. Did you know it was written by Rod Serling? Anyway, there's a small part for a doctor. Or I could just do some tech stuff behind the scenes."

Rod Serling. I didn't know he wrote *Requiem*. *Twilight Zone* had been a staple of my childhood. My sisters and I could recognize every episode by the first few eerie frames.

"I'm telling you it's a great play! Wow, this is fabulous." I hadn't met John yet, and wasn't getting real lessons, but it seemed serendipitous.

Two weeks later we were preparing for a jaunt to Scott's eldest sister's house in Massachusetts, to a wholesome household of colorful wallpaper, ceiling moldings, autumn centerpieces, and the general bustle of kid-raising in the era of computers, X-boxes, and music lessons, about as opposite from my childhood as you could get.

The night before our trip, the director of the community theater called to offer Scott the lead role in *Requiem*, that of the boxer, Mountain McClintock. Our whole trip was filled with the thrill of this new challenge. My sweet, discerning New-Age man, resistant to the cultural pressures for six-pack abs, was going to play an inarticulate brute.

Our first step was to rent any versions of *Requiem* we could find, which included a scratchy copy with Jack Palance as Mountain in the "Playhouse 90" version from television, one of a series of live dramas that set a high standard for early television. *Requiem* swept the 1956 Emmys, winning awards in all categories in which it was nominated, including best direction, best teleplay, and best actor. "Playhouse 90" established its reputation with this show. Then, for the film version, with Anthony Quinn cast in the title role, the writers changed Mountain's ethnicity because Quinn would not have been believable as a southern boy. Quinn modeled his wheezy grunt on the damaged voice of boxer Abie Bain, a Jewish light-heavyweight out of Newark, and then added cauliflower ears, swollen cheeks, and fake teeth for his transformation into the washed-up boxer. In truth, my father's "role" would have been the Maish part, Mountain's manager, a heavyset man in suspenders, tormented by the realities of life but full of a tender love for his young boxer. ("Fourteen years we worked together!") He smoked a cigar so stubby that his assistant, Army, Mountain's trainer, said "one inch closer and you'll be smoking your nose!" It was a play about relationships among men. When Mountain arouses the sympathies of a young female social worker, Maish blocks their relationship, deliberately failing to tell Mountain that Grace has called to offer him a new job interview in a different field.

As the weeks passed, I supported Scott in every way in his preparations. We "ran lines" together. I played every other role in his many scenes, so that he could work on his part. He easily perfected a Tennessee accent. We shopped for boxing robes, boxing shoes, boxing trunks, and 1950s pullover shirts and grey slacks at consignment shops. One day he announced that he would be shaving off all his facial hair, beard and mustache, and getting contact lenses. After all, a boxer couldn't wear glasses. Oh, and the long, lovely wavy hair would have to go too. It was 1950s all the way. We looked at images of boxers on the Internet.

Shaving day came. He spread out some newspapers over the bathroom sink to catch the clippings. I had done a little research on the *Queer Eye for the Straight Guy* site, and bought him a decent razor and gentle shaving cream. Once clean-shaven, the expressions around his mouth and chin revealed a boyish enthusiasm. His face looked so exposed and open. The range of expressions made me say, "I had no idea how much you loved me." It made me shy to look straight at him; I tilted my head down like a geisha.

I cupped his smooth face in my hands and stared into the sun. It was interesting. I rubbed my cheek against his, and we brushed our lips against each other lightly.

The haircut was next, and then we had to find retro clothes. One night, after four weeks of rehearsals, he had all the props and clothes together, and "Mountain" did a fashion show. I watched in amazement as a young Burt Lancaster loped into our living room, moving with authority and heft, not the Lancaster of *Elmer Gantry*, but maybe the Lancaster of *The Rainmaker*, another shuckster, but one with a loving heart. Scott-as-Mountain swung his arms lower. The 1950s-style pullover made him look bulkier.

"You fink," he bellowed. "You dirty fink, Maish! You dirty, lousy fink! . . . In all the dirty, crummy years I fought for you I never felt ashamed . . . I'd have gone into any ring bare-handed against a guy with a cleaver and that wouldn't have hurt me near as much as this."

I drew myself up, pretending to be a large and intimidating man like my father who pleads in desperation (he needs the money): "Do it for me, will you? Do it for me?"

My husband said: "And this is where I punch Army, you know, accidentally, because I'm really trying to hit Maish, but Army gets in the way."

"Are you really going to punch him?" *Would you even know how to do that?*

"No, but I gotta make it look realistic."

"Let me treat you to a private lesson with Jacob. He's not a professional boxer, but he could certainly teach the stance, and how you might throw a punch."

"Hey, that might be good," Scott said, shadowboxing, and jumping back and forth.

John would have of course been the better choice to mentor Scott, but he wasn't in our lives yet, and later, when John offered to teach Scott some defensive moves so we could box together, it was clear that Scott had absolutely no interest.

I was becoming a boxer, my husband was playing a boxer. You hear people talk about synchronicity: the experience of two or more causally unrelated events co-occurring as if there were a meaningful and underlying pattern at work. It's the topic of many a late-night conversation, and certainly material for spiritual contemplation. Is life a series of unconnected incidents or is there something larger?

What I do know is that the weird stone I'd turned over had skipped itself into a lake and wouldn't stop bouncing.

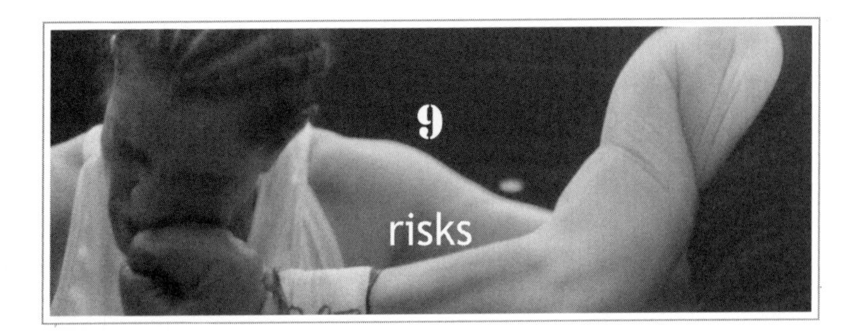

9
risks

Scott's theater performance was fantastic. I was excited, watching him stride across the stage. His friend Ken, sitting next to me, grabbed my hand as Mountain took the stage, hurt and bloody from a fight, and cried out, "It hurts, Maish, it hurts!" Scott as Mountain played a drunk scene, a love scene, and my favorite of all—a forceful physical scene when he grabs another manager's arm and holds it firmly. I had never seen such conviction and force come out of my gentle husband's being, and it was thrilling.

At the after-show cast party Scott was toasted and celebrated for his performance, with the group expressing hopes that Scott would return for future roles.

The comforting forest of his beard has returned.

Sometimes I miss Mountain, so I'll beg Scott to say a few lines with the Tennessee accent.

Lessons with John continued, as I learned to improve the jab, the right cross, the left hook, the hook to the body, the left uppercut, the right uppercut, the defensive maneuvers of slipping and weaving, and a trick called feinting. You act as if you're going to throw one punch and you surprise your opponent with another. The trickery was enormously satisfying. I couldn't wait for my lessons. When I didn't box, I felt a little down, restless. When I boxed, I was happier for the rest of the day.

After my boxing lessons, my arms sometimes felt heavy; my legs were tired, and sometimes my back hurt. But I never thought of stopping, and after a while the post-workout aches diminished. At least in the beginning.

"We ought to get you your own gloves," John said one day.

That signaled another phase—I felt myself bigger than life. I'd walk in the woods, in a state of happy ignorance, feeling strong, powerful, quick-footed; an animal primed to pounce if need be. Spotting a lone man near the lake, I'd think, *Could I take him? Where would I start? What punch would I use?* I'd stand in line at the bank, push my cart at the grocery store, and size people up. Not only was it somewhat absurd, I had little to back up my fantasies.

At a Golden Gloves tournament in Hubbard Park, Meriden, a few months later, I engaged in what I imagined to be informed ringside banter with a Marine Corps fighter who was waiting to box.

"Where are you from?" I asked cheerfully.

"Kenya," he replied, staring ahead.

"Ah. Yeah, I've been training with the ring announcer for eight months," I said, pointing to John. In other words, I'm an insider. How foolish he must have thought me.

"Hey! Could you move over?" Somebody's mother can't see her son in the ring. I was blocking the way, with my impostor body.

Then there was the day when I surprised myself with my behavior in a confrontation with a stranger. I had driven to the shoreline town of Milford to watch a film about the independent music scene at the local library. I had boxed with John that morning and it had gone extremely well. He had said, "good job, good job," several times, and "You're getting stronger." I felt light, happy.

The day was exquisite, sunny and cool. The film was a bit tedious, so I left early and happened upon an environmental fair with families, balloons, outdoor music. After the fair, I decided to go to my favorite café, only to find that parking was a nightmare. However, I spotted a small space on a street lined with boutiques. The enormous SUV in front was parked badly and inconsiderately, taking up more than one space, but I thought I could still fit my Subaru in. I pride myself on my parallel parking skills from my years living in New York City, and although I may have gently kissed the bumper of the car behind me, it was the most minor of pecks. It took a few maneuvers and corrections, but I squeezed in.

A woman and child burst out of a clothing store.

"Hey! Where are you going!? 'Cause you know, I won't be able to get out." She pointed to her huge vehicle, the one in front of me that had caused the original problem and made me struggle mightily to fit my car in.

"Well, you know, you did take up two spaces," I offered.

"Be that as it may," she sneered. "I need to get out. Wait five minutes and I'll be out."

Be that as it may. The phrase sounded disgustingly entitled. But, what the hell, I thought, and got back in my car to wait for her to emerge, so I could help her get out.

She finally comes out, shooting me some dirty looks as she drives away, and just as I'm leaving my car, thoughts of a chai tea latte and salad happily dancing in my head, two men approached their car, the one parked behind me.

Now a second woman emerged from the same store, stroller in tow.

"She hit your car! She hit your car! We saw the whole thing!"

Was Milford a hotbed of incensed and overwrought mothers? The men were suddenly up close and in my face, raging.

"Hey! You scratched the shit out of our car!"

This, before they had even looked at their bumper.

"Hang on, let's take a look," I said. For the life of me, I could not find a single scratch, perhaps just the faintest scuff of dust, maybe the size of a 1/8-inch piece of string.

"Look! Look!" They were practically jumping up and down. "It's scratched to shit!"

I figured they were probably coming from the nearby Stonebridge restaurant and bar. One of them, the more incensed and irrational, was inebriated or stoned. He was also the driver, it turned out.

"We want your information!" They screamed.

"Okay, let me get it." So I produced my license and registration, sad that this day, which had started out so delightfully, was descending into madness with strangers.

"I guess I'll take yours, too," I said. They proceeded to search the glove compartment, the visors, and under the seats. They couldn't find their information and suddenly looked sheepish.

"It's a rental car," one of them said.

"Oh, I can assure you—I've rented cars before—if there's a scratch smaller than a quarter, you're not responsible." I still didn't think I had seen a scratch, but I was overjoyed to have this kernel of information with which to calm them.

They were beginning to look crestfallen and shame-faced. The air was changing. I had them in the palm of my hand, as they say. *And I was getting my own boxing gloves*. And then the driver just couldn't resist.

"How the hell did you get into that space anyway?!"

"Why are you being such as aggressive prick?" I said. It had a projectile quality, like "Jacob would you teach me to box?," but not so innocent.

"Oh, so now you're calling me an aggressive prick?" He challenged.

Would this be it, I wondered, was there going to be physical violence? Maybe I should have just have called the police the minute they asked for my info and they didn't have theirs.

"Yes I am! I'm being very cooperative, and there's no need for you to be dealing with me in this manner."

The air changed again. It seemed I could have a real effect on the weather pattern. They backed down. I reassured them again that they would have no charges at the rental agency.

Bending down to the level of the driver, now behind the wheel, I could see his dilated pupils. I probably could have had him arrested.

"So be careful, okay? Life is short," I said.

"Well, you be careful, too," the driver said, and I thought he might be revving up again, but I let it go.

I was shaken. I had never spoken to a stranger that way before, no less in the wilds of the open street. And yet I had felt completely unafraid, completely justified, and quite empowered. It was such an odd experience. I sat down in a little park near the café and called my friend Kristin. Kristin was a tall woman who moved slowly and competently on life's conveyor belt and knew how to make yogurt, build a perfect fire, and size up people and situations with pithy, dead-on conclusions. We'd been friends for over twenty years. She was smart and irreverent. She had a "take no prisoners" approach when it came to dealing with difficult patients, from years of working with troubled war veterans. She'd often say, "you know, like us—middle-aged," languidly demonstrating her new golf swing, eager to age and be free of youth's unpredictability, happy to awaken me from the trance of life's highway, where I've gone past an alarming number of exits in a daze.

I expected a "Right on, sister!" from her about my Milford parking confrontation.

"What, um, is going on with you?" she asked.

"I don't know, I just don't want to take things anymore."

"Well . . . by using profanity you did descend to their level."

Damn it, she didn't get it. I was changing. I hadn't hit anyone, but it reminded me of how everyone who boxes, whether amateur or professional, shares and understands that certain feeling: *I like to hit and I know you like it, too.* Outside the boxing community the one question I can routinely count on is: *Why do you like it?*

Later that night I called John and told him the story.

"I'm proud of you," he said. "They were attacking you and you defended yourself. They were being jerks, and they had nothing to back it up. Good girl."

Some years back, I briefly wore a fragment of a testosterone patch the size of a puzzle piece to help with menopausal symptoms. My sister Susan swore it made me more aggressive. I'd come home, crack open a cold beer, and call her up and complain about something.

Menopause and its treatments are long over, and I don't think the scene in the little suburb of Milford would have played the same if I had kept doing sit-ups on an exercise ball and never taken up boxing.

"So, John," I asked at our next lesson, "is there a period for us middle-aged women—I know you teach a bunch of us—you know, a phase where you feel like . . ."

"You mean where you're thinking: who am I? When you're looking at other people differently?"

"Yes! Absolutely. I just feel like . . . what am I becoming? It's so disorienting."

We circle each other like predators, working on my left uppercut. I'm frustrated because I don't seem to have any strength. I throw one, and it's wide, wild and ridiculous. Suddenly, I let out a huge burp.

John laughs. "It's okay," he says, "we don't stand on ceremony here. Body noises, smells, blood . . ."

"Right, soon I'll be spitting into a bucket."

"Hey, I've had fighters throw up in the ring."

"John, why do they call it a ring anyway? It's a square!" I said.

"Ah, well, a few hundred years ago, they drew a circle in the sand and they fought inside it. Then, years later, in the bare-knuckle days, they held a rope in a circle."

From the barbell area of the gym comes a deep and satisfied masculine grunt and the sound of weights crashing to the floor.

John's grunts were plentiful and complex, like all the Eskimo words for snow. There was the grunt of pleasure when I hit well, the grunt of "what the hell was that!" when I panicked and flailed, the warning grunt, the grunt of admiration, the grunt of satisfaction, the "Nooooo!" when I did something really stupid, as if I were a fly and he was swatting me away, followed by the disparaging crease of his disappointed mouth.

"C'mon, snap it! That's not sexy! You're flailing!" I thwacked and pivoted, danced and weaved. He went on, never winded.

"Okay, hold on, let me show you something. If you move your arm back before the cross, I'm gonna see it coming and you're gonna wake up in the locker room. You ever see people in a barroom fight? You know, it's like they wind up their right hand like they're gonna throw a pitch. You can see it coming a mile away. If I see it coming, you're mine. Keep your arm close to your body. That's it, baby, you got it."

Wake up in the locker room. What a bizarre notion, and someone was actually saying that to me, as if it were a possibility for my future that I had to guard against. The only barroom fights I'd seen were in movies or on television.

"You know what, John," I say, at the end of my tenth three-minute round. "You've brought me more physical joy than I've had in a long time." It just popped out, another projectile (they were happening more and more), as if the sweat, the gym, and the passion of the sport had lubricated my verbal flow. Boxing was so intimate, from the tender swaddling of my hands by a man I hardly knew to his acceptance of my body's struggles as I tried to learn, improve, and, I suppose, impress.

"Careful," he laughed. "That's what my girlfriend says."

Ah, such confidence.

I left the gym that day thinking about what it would be like to have John's confidence. Women's confidence is often dependent on physical attractiveness, while men can project myriad qualities that magnetize people to them. John was no Adonis, but women were drawn to his openness, his virility, and, yes, his cockiness and humor.

John had recently lent me a book about boxer Barney Ross. He had these qualities, too. "Back on Independence Boulevard" (a fancy neighborhood, especially for successful Jews back in the 1930s, west of the Maxwell Street ghetto in Chicago), he wrote, "I was cock of the walk." What would he think of me and what could I say to him? I wanted that confidence. I opened the door to my Subaru and started the engine, imagining he was in the passenger seat looking at me.

"Where we goin' baby?" His voice was a little husky.

I look over at Barney—"Beryl the Terrible," "One Punch Rasofsky," Champion of the World in the Lightweight, Junior Welterweight, and Welterweight divisions from 1933 to 1938. He was adorable, if you could say that about a champ. Thick bushy eyebrows, like those on my father in an early photograph taken before the war, as he leaned against a small plane, jaunty in a thick turtlenecked sweater. Barney also had an impish smile, and slicked-back dark wavy hair.

"Barney, I can't believe it's really you," I said, feeling shy and flirty at the same time.

The sun speared through the gap in his top teeth, and he grinned. "So I heard you say your dad liked the ponies. You know how I got into all that? Al Jolson! He took me to Arlington Park, Chicago."

He pronounced it "Tchi-cawgo"—just the way my dad did, like the sound of a disapproving crow.

"But I never could pick a winner. After a while Mr. Jolson didn't even want me near him. He said stay away! He didn't want to get the curse. The bookies liked me, though. How'd your dad do?"

"Not so great, either. Small gains—then he'd blow it on dinner."

"Aw, my kind of gent! You were a lucky little lady."

"I suppose," I murmured, remembering my father pushing food away and glowering. I tried to focus on the turn I was making onto the busy Post Road.

"Cmon! Keep your chin up, whatsa madda? You got troubles? Let me tell you a story. When Itchik, my father, god rest his soul, came over here, he didn't have anything . . . they called him Isadore, more American-like . . ."

"Barney! Isadore was my grandfather's name, too!" I said. "And my other grandfather was Barney—I was named after him." I had always been told that I was named "Binnie" because my father admired an actress named "Binnie Barnes," a swashbuckling blonde heroine in old movies. Years later he met her on a plane and she signed an 8 × 10 glossy "To Binnie from Binnie—it's been a lucky name for me." A sweet-faced older lady smiles out at me from under a parasol. A few years ago that same face gazed at me from the obituary page in the *New York Times*.

But there was also the other story: that I was named in recognition of my father's father, who had died long before I was born—his name was Barney. "If you were born a boy, we were going to call you Benny. *If you were a boy*. So the name Benny came before the name Binnie. They must have wanted a boy, after my two older sisters. They were all set for that, name picked out and everything.

"You see that? We're like family—and you're feeling better already, aren'tcha?" He took off his white fedora and brushed off a few stray dots of dust. "Benny—that's a special name you know, because of Benny Leonard. Don't forget him. He gave us everything."

I continued to drive and he continued with his story. The greasy smell of Brylcreem permeated my car. I guess Barney didn't believe in the old slogan "A little dab'll do ya"—he must have used the whole tube on that helmet of dark hair.

". . . like I was sayin', he had nothing. There was pushcarts. My mother, god rest her, too, was from Poland."

"My mother, too, a shtetl," I said.

"I'm never gonna get this out, am I? Jes' kidding you, you're a good egg. But when I was two we got on the train and went to Chicago. My mother's uncle had a store there. What a scene, the smells and sounds and crowds. We didn't have much, but I loved the action, you know what I mean? And there was nothing like the taste of the cholont, only on Shabbas of course. My mother's hands would be raw from peeling the potatoes. But that's not the thing, the thing I want to tell you. I heard you say about your dad, and the Murder, Inc goons, well I got caught up, too. The thing is, it was action, but it was you know . . . the usual . . . in the neighborhood . . . we were roaming around, unsupervised, so what do ya get? Gangs!" He reached into the pocket of his suitjacket and pulled out a gold-tipped toothpick.

"I roamed around, too, in Newark, but I was just looking for boys," I said sheepishly.

"Well, with me it was rough. They called us scheenies. I heard it all—'kill the dirty little Jew,' that kind of thing. They wouldn't let us swim in the pool so we got physical. Then I'd come on home and my father, the rebbe, he'd see the bruises and he would get out the leather cat-o-nine tails . . . I got beat even worse at home. So you know I stole, I gambled, everything, fights on the streets."

"I didn't have anything like that, Barney. So I don't know why I box, but you . . ." The traffic on the Post Road was congesting in that sudden way it often did—cars battling for their turns into Trader Joe's, TGIF, and other chain retailers and restaurants. It was hard to stay focused on what Barney was saying. I kept thinking about the names. Benny, Barney, Binnie. *Odd.*

"Well, I know you're a psychologist; I thought you might be interested, you know, in what started the boxing really. I had four before me, they all died. Me, I wasn't so strong either. Asthma. My tate was a Talmud scholar, a rebbe. He started on the Lower East Side, but couldn't make it there. We had family in Chicago, West Side. I lived in a tenement flat on top of a fish market. Barely two rooms. Hundreds of families shared one bathtub, can you imagine? Anyway, my father opens this grocery store, see, across the street. I was to become a Hebrew teacher; that was his dream. I wasn't that much of a *trumbenik* until . . ." He paused, and took a silk handkerchief out of his pants pocket. The letters B and R were monogrammed in deep red.

I knew what was coming. I had read about it.

"First I heard the shot, then my Pa yelling. I was fourteen, and they broke into the grocery store, hoods, you know? They took everything from the cash register and then . . . they shot him . . . I saw him on the floor, my father. There was blood. They'd killed him. And after that my mother, she . . . wasn't the same. They put her in the hospital. I couldn't do anything for her. Me and Morrie, my brother, were sent to cousin Henry, and the others, the others, they were . . . well, the orphanage. I clenched my fists right then and there and made a personal vow to get them out. And you know what? It made me a better fighter. Every time I fought, I pictured it, kicking Pa's murderers until they screamed in agony."

"What a senseless, horrible crime," I said. I reached out to touch his shoulder but his hand went up reflexively and caught mine in a grip.

"Ow!" I recoiled.

"Pardon me, I just, when I remember I'm back there. You meant well. Well, hey, this is no joke today, huh? I just wanted to tell you this. You're intelligent."

I wanted to change the subject. "Is it true? About you and Al Capone?"

"That's a turn! Capone and I, we were close. He knew everything about my life, what happened to my family, everything. Yes, he was ruthless, but with me he was kind. I did some jobs for him, but this is how he was kind, you see, he told me to beat it, he gave me money to leave the mob. He insisted. He didn't want that life for me."

I could tell Barney was feeling better after spilling the details of his childhood trauma. He was flicking his toothpick between his thumb and forefinger.

"For a while I gave up all the Jewish things. You know, I'd taught Hebrew. But I just couldn't anymore; I didn't think there was a God. I did say Kaddish three times a day, out of respect for Pa. But the next year it was boxing, all the way. I gotta tell ya, though, Ma couldn't know. You know my real name?"

"Beryl, right?" I said tentatively.

"Hey, you're all right! Beryl Rasofsky. I had to hide it, the boxing, from my Ma—I took on Barney Ross. Didn't go stupid like Mushy Callahan. We couldn't have our mothers knowing we were fighting," Ross said.

"Wow. I thought Mushy was adding the Irish name to avoid the anti-Semitism," I said.

"Nah. I mean not that there wasn't anti-Semitism. It was his Ma. But my Ma found out. To her it was horrible. It made me a . . . a bum. But you know, it saved my life, boxing. I wrote something, let me see." He fumbled in his breastpocket and pulled out a cocktail napkin.

"Here we go: It wasn't long before I could feel my chest expanding, my hands hardening, my body toughening and my mind growing sharper."

"That is beautiful. Seriously, I love that. I feel sharper too," I said.

"Anyway, I got to be going," Barney smoothed out his hat. "I could talk all day to you, young lady. You're a good listener. But I gotta head out to Grossinger's—they got it all decked out for me as a training retreat. You ever been up there? It's Ferndale, New York. They got everything there. Runyon's coming up to write it up. They're all watching me. I'm kind of, you know, the center of it all. You oughta come up sometime. I'm real worried, though. I been reading in the papers about problems in Germany for our people. They're boycotting our businesses. It's grim, I tell ya. What do you think, Mrs., what do you think is going to happen with this Hitler guy?"

I pulled over to let him out at Jacob Marley's, thinking he might enjoy a drink. He liked that sort of thing, and wasn't training just yet.

"I don't know, Barney." We looked at each other. The bushy eyebrows were making a less perky shape, and the tough guy looked worried. "Have a great fight!" I called out as he shut the car door.

"*Gezinterhayt*, Mrs.," he said, walking backward while he spoke. "Don't forget Benny. He was a real scientist. I was, what, fourteen when they shot Pa but I remember—it was just a few months after that Benny Leonard fought Lew Tendler—that was July 1923. Anyway, it was a real pleasure talking with ya."

There he was, "Beryl the Terrible," studying the menu outside the restaurant, his hands in his pockets, leaning forward and rocking back and forth on his heels. The crease in his white pants was still crisp as if he'd never sat inside the car.

Eleven days before Barney Ross's fight, at a rally in Madison Square Garden for George Washington's birthday, twenty thousand people wearing swastikas goose-stepped outside in big black boots. They shouted "Sieg Heil!"

Back at the Grossinger's camp Beryl Rasofsky read the continuing bad news from Germany and wrote later that it had strengthened his resolve to fight "like I was fighting for all my people."

Ross became hugely successful as a lightweight boxer; his fights brought huge crowds, big purses for the time, and an entourage of celebrities. He is sometimes ranked with baseball's Hank Greenberg as the most admired Jewish athlete in America. He retired from boxing in 1938 and, at age thirty-two, enlisted in the U.S. Army after the Pearl Harbor attack. In the battle of Guadalcanal, Ross sustained serious injuries while rescuing his comrades from a Japanese ambush. He won a silver star for heroism.

Perhaps his greatest contributions ultimately came through political activism. He was a well-known supporter of the Emergency Committee to Save the Jewish People of Europe. He was outspoken—criticizing the allies' apathy toward the Holocaust, and assisting on a committee to rescue Jews. The Jewish prizefighters' legacy often extended outside the ropes of the boxing ring.

Barney may never have gotten over the traumatic losses of his early life, and certainly spent plenty of time trying to self-medicate his pains, both physical and emotional. He did beat his addictions finally. The great 1948 boxing film *Body and Soul* had been commissioned by actor John Garfield (a boxer himself who starred in the title role) to depict the life of Barney Ross, but Hollywood moguls, worried about the taint of the addictions, disguised the details. You can feel him in the story, though. In another film, in 1957, *Monkey on My Back*, Cameron Mitchell plays Barney Ross and it's all about addiction. Ross reportedly hated the film, and I can understand why—it's a curiously flat story with none of Ross's troubled childhood in it. It's Barney the boxer, then Barney the irrepressibly optimistic and stubborn gambler, then an agonizingly long war sequence, and then Barney the morphine addict.

Barney Ross got a small part in a production of *Requiem for a Heavyweight.* "The Pride of the Ghetto" died in his hometown of Chicago, at the age of fifty-seven. His first wife's name was Pearl Siegel. *Siegel.* My mother's maiden name.

Brylcreem lost its popularity in the 1960s, when men began to prefer a drier look for their hair.

10

siblings

When you visit your therapist, you may maintain the fiction for a time that you are the only patient, until the inevitable day you see someone else in the waiting room. Or you strain to hear the muffled words of the previous patient through the door, and you wonder if they are more interesting, or more crazy, or more special than you. When they come out, you want to but you can't look them right in the eye, like you can't stare directly at the sun. John made me feel like I was the only student in the world when he was teaching me. I hadn't reached the logical conclusion that he must make others feel that way, too.

The first boxing sibling I met was Jenni. I arrived at my lesson just as a perky and petite woman was walking out of John's office. He introduced us—she'd been boxing with him for two years, and they had just sparred. That means they had donned headgear, both wore gloves, and then, well, hit each other. I was immediately envious and competitive. They were sparring; we were not.

"If you ever get the chance to hit a man," Jenni said conspiratorily as she packed up her gym bag, "do it! And do it hard."

"And she did very well sparring today, too!" John shouted. "Hey rabbit," he added, "give me a few minutes—I gotta make some calls."

"I'm a foster kid," Jenni announced, pulling up a stool next to me at the counter where the showgirl sold the power bars. "So I'm a natural fighter. Plus my own mother was bipolar. I got the beatings when she was angry."

I made a quick adjustment to Jenni's style. She was open, eager, devoid of all pretense. Her eyes fixed on me with intensity and a hunger to connect. My eyes dropped to a small cross hanging around her neck. I felt like adopting her myself.

"Yup, I'm a good Christian woman, peaceful, loving, devout—and I love to box!"

"Were you always athletic and active as a child?" I asked.

"Oh yes! Rock climbing, bike-riding, roller skating, running, baseball, football, weightlifting, jazz dancing, tried ballet but got kicked out for being a klutz, or so they said. You want some tea? I think tea is great!" She popped up and pressed the button on a hot water dispenser.

"I'm going to get a chai tea latte at Starbucks afterwards," I said. It was my ritual.

"Oh, 500 calories, right there!" she declared.

This was exactly what I didn't want from my gym experiences—prohibitions, warnings, deprivation.

"But you're boxing now, so it's okay" she added.

"I'm epileptic," she blurted out. "The doctors wanted to put me in a bubble. The teachers didn't want me to play sports but I did anyway. I did all of it."

I wasn't sure I had heard her correctly. And I was worried about my ankle? Jenni picked up on my surprise.

"That's right. Diagnosed when I was five years old. I had my first seizure when my mom smacked me in the tub and I hit my head and went out. I was three. Or if I'd have a high fever, it would happen. My seizures are triggered by pain. Nobody knew my mother beat me until I was twelve years old. She threw me across the room in front of the entire family at Thanksgiving."

"Wow," I couldn't think of anything more intelligent or precise to say. "But with boxing, aren't you afraid of . . ."

"Having a seizure? Well, if I know how much pain is coming, I can control it, I can take the hit. When I'm boxing with John, yes, there is a chance he will hit me. It's just that the better you can prepare your body to take the pain, the better you can control how fast the pain stimuli travels up to your brain. A seizure happens when it goes from one neuron to another. If it goes too fast, you get a seizure until it reconnects."

The water dispenser beeped and I tried to integrate this epilepsy lesson as she selected a zero-calorie chamomile tea bag from a basket.

"And the thing is—this stepfather, who was a pedophile, let me take karate and dance class. He paid for the lessons! I couldn't join team sports because it would involve a teacher or a coach. And from thirteen to twenty I was seizure free!"

She practically sang out the statement.

"God gave me a break."

"So is it gone?" I asked, tentatively.

"No. At twenty-one it came back full force. I had three seizures in six months, in public, grand mal seizures. But you know what? My body was good about it. I knew it was coming. So tired afterwards. As a little girl they would give me caffeine and chocolate, tea and candy. I didn't know anyone else with epilepsy. It was a stigma, you know, so no one talked about it."

"How did you meet John?" I was enjoying and admiring Jenni, but her story was definitely messing with my fiction that John was all mine. Still, there was no turning back now. I supposed it must be different for the more usual team sports where everyone shares the coach.

"A few years ago I was exercising at Fit World. I saw him boxing with women. I asked him how much he charged and asked if I could take lessons. He asked me why I wanted to learn. I said I wanted to learn something new."

"What did you think of it?" I asked, remembering my trembling hands after the workout.

"I couldn't lift a fork. But I couldn't wait to go back."

We laughed.

"You can be a strong boxer and still be feminine," she went on. "Because femininity is about confidence."

"Do you think other women boxers feel that way?" I asked.

"Yes! I know I liked it right away. There was an immediate rush, leather hitting leather. And I was allowed to hit. I wasn't causing anyone pain, either. I found out that boxing is about control, manner, and etiquette. You can be an animal in the ring, but without the gloves you can't touch each other. There are rules. I wished my mother had done it; you know, found a place to put her anger or dilute it. Maybe then I wouldn't have been her punching bag."

Jenni paused, and wiped a tear from her eye.

"John taught me to get out of my mother's way."

I reached for her hand and gave it a squeeze.

The boxing community was so open; the people I was meeting seemed unpretentious, welcoming, warm, and not what I would have expected.

"Have you sparred yet?" Jen's tears had disappeared. I shook my head. "You will. The first time we sparred I saw the glove come at me and I froze. John knew I had epilepsy but he didn't know I had been beaten. This gave it away. I saw my mother standing in front of me. 'Oh shit,' I said, and ducked and hid. I was embarrassed. John said, 'You gotta learn to take a hit, you gotta get over this. Jen, I'm comin' at ya.' I had to learn to take those punches, but on my own terms."

This was a radical idea—to get over the trauma of being hit, learn to anticipate and actually take a hit—invert the power, take the power back. It was like women who had been sexually assaulted and then took up martial arts.

"Is John like a father to you?" I asked.

"No. Brother! He's like a brother—hey, there he is, I'm going to take off!" Jenni scooped up her gym bag.

John had finally emerged from his office, and we began our walk toward our boxing corner.

"Do you spar with all your patients, I mean clients?" I asked John as we began our lesson. Jenni had asked if I had sparred yet. I was dying to ask John if we would ever spar, but I had automatically instituted a "don't ask, don't tell" policy about my training. I didn't want to know if I was ready or if I wasn't, I didn't want to know if I should be doing aerobics or weight training, I just awaited my orders. I was letting an authority figure (perhaps the only male one in my life) completely lead the way.

"Oh no—sometimes you don't even get to the stage of sparring because it's not the physicality of it, it's the emotional . . . ," John said.

"The what?"

"I mean they can only do it if they don't think I'm angry at them. I can be a scary guy. Of course they don't think they are supposed to hit anyone, let alone a 200-pound man coming at them."

"Is that just with women?" I arranged my array of liquids in the cup holders of a treadmill, removing their tops. I'd been experimenting lately with the best place to put them.

"Get over here, rabbit, put your gloves up," John said. "With men they're more afraid of the humiliation . . . they're not so much afraid you're angry at them, but that they have to relinquish complete control to another man. And you know I train my women exactly the same as I train my men. You're getting professional boxing training, my little diva of destruction, just as if you were going to compete."

So I'm not going to compete? *Don't ask, don't tell.*

"I think," I said, panting, "that women are kind of used to not having control, you know, despite the gains of feminism and all, and men have it. And maybe that's a good experience for a man to have at some point in his life, not having it. And vice versa."

Thwack! My right cross was improving. John grunted with pleasure. "Geez, you're cerebral," he said.

I hoped he didn't think that was a liability. I had put all my eggs into the intellectual basket for so long, and as someone (either Mark Twain or Andrew Carnegie, no one can decide) once said, "Put all your eggs in one basket . . . and watch that basket."

"Well, remember, I'm a Jewish boxer! I'm a scholar!"

"Yes, my little divaleh of destruction. I don't know about not having control being good for men, anyway," he said. "We've become a nation of wimps. I don't have much use for men, to tell you the truth. Every time I meet one, and he hears what I do, I've got to listen to the posturing and bragging about their football days or how they got in a fight once. It bores me to death."

Now I have my goal. Sparring will up the ante, and it's doable, when I'm ready. It is not even an attempt to defeat an opponent. It is the working on mastering a certain type of technique that is part of the overall repertoire. The sparring sessions are not "bouts," but they give you an opportunity to try things out. Oriental martial arts, following Bruce Lee's popularity, borrowed the term and added weapons practice, and it came to be associated with engaging in fighting sessions, but really it's still training. What's essential is that the punch mitts won't be my targets and there will be some light blows.

I want to spar, like Jenni.

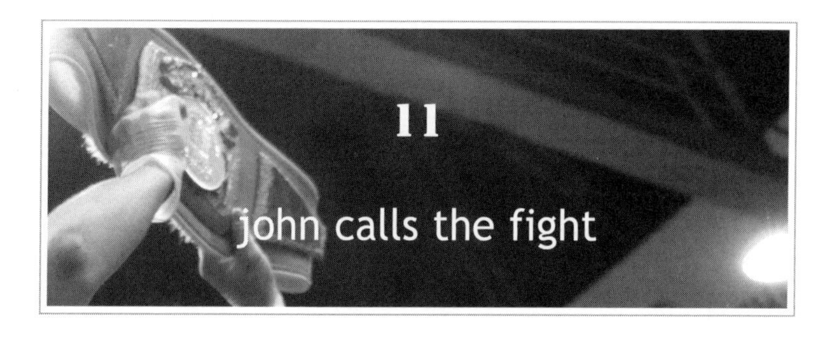

11

john calls the fight

I was having a difficult time with a close friend who was going through a marital crisis and had recently entered psychoanalysis. It was an odd mixture of events: she talked little about the problems with her soon-to-be ex-husband and more about being absolutely certain she was in love with her new analyst, and that her dearest hope was that he would return her affection. Gently, I tried to remind her about the concept of transference, but she insisted vigorously that this was different. I tried to be patient and supportive, even as she began to smother me with an intrusive batch of needs and criticisms. Her moods were increasingly mercurial. She lost at least twenty-five pounds in five minutes, and began wearing short skirts and tight shiny pants. She sat differently, legs tucked underneath, or pretzel-style. My empathy for her situation was strong—she was going through a major life transition that made her act like a teenager. I'd seen people respond to divorce in some similar ways, and kept thinking how awful it must be to be facing so much loss.

But telephone conversations had become marathons, and her tone was increasingly accusative. "You like Kristin more than you like me." "You don't care about me." And one particularly cryptic comment: "You're defended against the erotic and I don't like that about you!" And this when I was sick in bed with the flu. I couldn't keep up; I felt battered. Who wanted to hear nuanced versions of your personality flung at you while you were dripping into a box of tissues? It was grade school drama mixed with unwanted psychoanalytic interpretations.

I tired to chalk these attacks up to her volatile state, but her disappointments in me were vast, endless. It seemed I could never do enough. I began to dread seeing her; this was a very vexing loss—I had long valued her unique mind and her friendship. Whenever I did try to process the difficulties with her, it only got worse and we wandered into a quagmire of recriminations and misunderstandings.

One morning at my house (we sometimes boxed there) John noticed that my jab was pathetically weak. He had a way of diagnosing my state of being by my first punch, which was always a jab. He'd sometimes ask: "Are you okay?" I'd say "Sure," and he'd ask, "Are you telling me the truth?"

"I'll tell you why my jab is weak," I said. Out came the story of my friend's criticisms of me, my fatigue, my concern about her, my frustration. He reached out and put his arm around me. It was a pristine hug, side against side, and I felt the warmth and tenderness of his being. I sobbed against his chest. My gloved hands lay limp at my sides. I imagined John reassuring his children. It was embarrassing to realize I envied them.

"You're a magnificent woman," he said. "Don't worry about her; you can't fix her. She's being ridiculous."

We stood for an eternity, rocking against each other. He gently stroked one side of my arm. I knew he would have stood with me like that for as long as I needed. Suddenly I knew I was crying for more than just my friend's bullying. I wished my father had protected me in a different way. I wished my life had gone differently. I wished I'd found boxing earlier. *Happiness reminds me of sadness.*

"John, this is weird, but can I tell you something?"

"Anything."

What a good shrink.

"When I was around fourteen, this thing happened in Newark. Black families were moving into the neighborhood, buying up all the houses really fast. One by one, on our street behind the high school, we watched the change in the neighborhood. The mostly Jewish families were fleeing to the suburbs. In fact, it was called "the White Flight." We didn't have the money to go, and actually my family, and I'm proud of this, didn't feel any need to move. My family wasn't particularly racist. So when our place was sold to a Jamaican family, and they said they didn't need the second-floor apartment and they would rent to us, we planned on staying."

"One day I was walking along Chancellor Avenue to go to Halem's for an egg cream and a comic book, and a car pulled up. I recognized the Jamaican guy. I can still see his round face and easy smile. He offered me a ride. I didn't want to seem rude to our new prospective landlord, so I got in. He began asking me questions about school. Everything seemed innocent enough. Then he asked if I had a boyfriend. I mumbled some vague answer. 'Do you think you and me could go out sometime?' he asked. I said 'I don't think my mother would like that.' I was afraid; this was going bad and I had to get out of the car.

"He reached over and stroked my long hair, which fell across my breast, saying 'Gee, you have some pretty hair.' His hand had touched my breast and was lingering there. I urged him to let me get out of the car, and finally I was able to get out. I ran home and cried in my room. My thoughts were crazed—how could we stay in the house with this man there—I would be in danger all the time—but how could we move—Daddy would be mad—we had no money—we couldn't go to Maplewood or Short Hills—the fancy suburbs—Mommy needed to be near a grocery store—but how could I avoid him? I was in a circle of despair. Telling my parents didn't seem like a possibility. That next weekend my sister Susie came home from college. She got the story out of me and said I absolutely must tell them."

"Did your Dad go after the guy?" John asked.

"No. It wasn't like that, I mean it was even worse in a way. I got up the courage to tell my father, and you know what he said?"

I tried to ignore how much my back hurt from standing for so long, because I didn't want to move from John's comforting arms.

"What, baby?"

"Shit!" That's what my father said. 'So where the hell do you want to move?' He was angry, but he was angry at me, as if I'd done something wrong. He never confronted the guy. Then he continued to insist that the decision about where the family would move was now up to me. It's funny—a colleague and I were swapping childhood stories once, and she said, 'Well, at least he knew you had to move.' Sometimes I think therapists who have kids are forever defending the parents. And maybe we who haven't are more apt to identify with the children. But, anyway, my father chose to make me the responsible one. I opened up the Sunday *New York Times* real estate section and found a listing for a spanking new garden apartment complex in Fords, New Jersey, a god-awful place near main roads so my father could get to Newark Airport easily, and across the street from the A&P, so my mother could shop. It was the beginning of decline—my mother didn't do well there, got even more isolated, and I went from a diverse high school to John F. Kennedy Memorial High School, where I was one of three Jews. There was one black student and he was president of the junior class. Those two years there were miserable."

"Baby, I'm so sorry. I think I've gone too far the other way," John said. "I punched one of my daughter's boyfriends in the face. I think I broke his nose. Actually I'm not proud of it. Not at all."

"I don't know—I think I would have preferred that."

I reached up with a glove to blot my tears. My father had confronted the gym teacher and the swim counselor in his erratic "leave my daughter alone" way, but, when it came to an unwanted hand on my breast and a further threat of sexual assault, he blamed me and sulked. Maybe he was afraid he would kill the guy. Either way, should a fourteen-year-old girl be given the responsibility to pick the next place for her family to live?

"I'm calling the fight," John said gently but firmly.

"What do you mean?"

"That's it. You're done with that so-called friend for now. I'm calling the fight. I can't have my fighter hurt."

Of course it wasn't up to John, but the relief was both symbolic and extraordinary. I had tried; I had given it my all, but I was getting hurt and he was stopping the fight. I couldn't believe I had discovered such an ally in such an unlikely place, and I didn't feel I had taken a pass, or had wriggled out of something I needed to face.

We didn't box that day. We sat on the sofa and talked about our childhoods, our vulnerabilities, our sense of not ever truly fitting in. In truth, we had a lot in common. We were such an odd pair, I thought. I never would have discovered a friend like John if I hadn't learned to box. I would have seen a man like him out in the world and given him a wide berth—we would probably not even have made eye contact.

And when it was time for John to leave my house, we noticed something unusual on the floor—tufts of white stuffing were strewn everywhere like little puffy clouds. They'd been yanked out of throw pillows by Griffin and Sabine, who were probably upset that I'd been crying.

"I guess they were working something out, too," he said, stuffing the equipment into his red mesh bag and heading out to his truck. John had two chubby pugs at home. One was named Dempsey.

Several months later, in the front seat of that very truck, John confided some personal stresses to me. He let loose a few tentative tears while I held him and murmured reassurances. "Boys don't cry," he protested. I wasn't throwing punches, but my arms felt particularly strong as I wrapped them around his neck and told him everything would be all right. I could see that it had been extremely important for John not to need anyone, and that's part of what drew him to boxing.

Heather Byer wrote in *Sweet: An Eight-Ball Odyssey* about her own weird stone—learning to play competitive pool after years in the film industry. "What do I have in common with a tormented guy like Trevor? . . . why do I desire, at age thirty-two, to surround myself with human wrecks who exhibit occasional bursts of beauty?" she wonders.

There's an empty pace in her life that is somehow filled by the odd personalities, the off-color jokes, the sights and sounds and smells of the pool halls.

I know just how she feels.

John's dad was also a traveling salesman, mostly selling textbooks to schools and public libraries, but while my dad was embittered, John's was ferocious. His parents met at a religious order. Emil, John's father, was becoming a Dominican friar and Ada, John's mother, was becoming a cloistered nun. Instead they fell in love and got married and had two sons; John was the firstborn, Mark the second.

Like my mother, John's mother Ada wanted him home with her. She claimed she was afraid John would get hurt, so she didn't want him to play any sports—no baseball, no football, nothing. A lot of the early Jewish boxers' mothers shared Ada's fear. They were terrified their sons would get hurt. When successful lightweight Maxie Shapiro left the house to go fight, he lied to his mother about his bag of equipment—he claimed it was full of ties and that he was a salesman. There was another aspect to parents' views of their Jewish sons fighting: *shanda*. Education was so highly prized and fighting might make you seem like a bum. In *His People*, a silent film made in 1925, a mother expresses her disgust about her son's becoming a boxer: "A Box-fyteh? So that's what you become? For this we came to America? Better you should be a gangster or even a murderer. The shame of it. A Box-fyteh!"

When John could get out of his mother's clutches, he did try football in junior high, but hated it.

"It was bullshit violence," he said.

To keep John and his brother Mark with her, Ada claimed she had cancer, heart attacks, rare blood disorders. "Willie, you tell them," his mom would say dramatically, whipping up yet another tale of dying, always crying wolf, and nothing ever came to anything.

Willie was not John's father. He was a young kid who came on the scene during the period when John's dad had enough of his wife's alcoholism and craziness and moved to Buffalo. John's mother often had kids in the house while Dad was traveling. In those years she was a hippie mom, with kids smoking dope in the house with her. Willie stayed on and became her lover. John would introduce him to people as his brother because it was so embarrassing; he was closer to John's age (only seven years older) than his mother's. It seemed like a fine plan until one night John came home with some friends and his "brother" and mother were on the couch. John's friends were direct: "Did we just see your brother screwing your mother?" After that John stopped bringing anyone home. John claimed he didn't think anything of Willie—"It was like my mother had a pet; this computer geek." She badgered him, and it took some heat off the boys. "He had no balls; he didn't stand up to her, and wouldn't stick up for us, but he became her major whipping boy."

I remember a story about my half-brother Gary that my eldest sister Mikki told me. Sometimes our father would take Mikki along in the bakery truck in Brooklyn and they would pick up Gary, who was introduced as her cousin. She wasn't told until much later that Gary was in fact her brother.

One time John's father caught Ada in bed with Willie and proceeded to throw him down the stairs.

I once awoke in my room in that apartment in Fords, New Jersey, to the terrifying and unfamiliar sounds of a scuffle in the next room. My father, enraged with the way my brother-in-law was treating my eldest sister, had thrown him against the wall. Their entire relationship was full of traumatic triggers for my father because at least ten years before they married, my sister and her husband lived together. This was still shocking then, and it must have evoked the scandal of my parents' own taboo love affair. I covered my ears with a pillow, praying for the sounds in the next room to stop.

John and I both had troubled mothers, but while mine was quiet in her depression, John's was loud and vicious. She had the gift to drive you crazy, to get under your skin and stay there. She needled everyone with incessant ranting—comments like "You and your brother are gay, you're not my children, I spent endless hours in labor for you, you're worthless, nothing, I wish I had real men as sons."

She floated from job to job, mostly clerical, developing delusions about why she was fired. The Mafia was trying to kill her. Everyone was trying to have sex with her. That's what happened to her job at Rogers Foam, a company in the north end of Hartford. John liked it when she worked there because the guys would give him and his brother little foam couches and pillows, which they brought home and set up as furniture. That image of those troubled boys setting up a room with small furniture makes me want to weep.

They moved twenty-seven times. Mother wouldn't pay the bills or she'd cause fights, and they would get evicted. The closest thing to protection John ever felt was when Mom would come to school and stick up for him. The only thing he remembers her telling him: "It doesn't matter how bad it is, as long as you tell the truth I will defend you whether you were right or wrong." He appreciated that sentiment, and she went to bat for him at school when he got violent, but even that was tainted because John felt it was in her best interests to make sure he didn't get sent away. Her motivating drive was that she didn't want to lose her boys. John felt she saw them as her servants or playmates.

It reminded me of my mother writing the excuse notes for my many absences. She wanted me home with her.

John got into a lot of fights. Because he was so much bigger, other kids would be aiming to build their rep by picking on him. He was reasonably kind-hearted, but if you messed with him, he had enough anger to kill anything in the room even without knowing how to fight. "I was willing, more than willing," he told me.

"John, do you remember your dreams?" I asked one day, while trying to position a right uppercut to meet his chin.

"Not too much—they're pretty scary."

"What do you mean?"

"They're always situations where I'm out of control."

"You mean like going wild?"

"No, I mean where I'm in an awful situation and there's absolutely nothing I can do about it. I'm helpless."

John tells me he doesn't have physical fears. He learned early on that anything that happens typically heals. "My demons are not physical," he said.

John's dad was a fantastic swimmer and great basketball player, very athletic. His approach was: Throw them into the water; it'll toughen them up. Maybe that's what I had needed. The theory was if they don't drown, they'll be swimming, and John admired that devil-may-care attitude. "That's how dads should be," John told me once. "Especially if you're going to be a dad to boys. Coddling boys doesn't serve them well as men. It makes them become pushovers."

It couldn't be more different from my dad, who didn't have faith in my physical prowess; he threatened others who did.

He probably thought we'd both drown if I got into the water.

Boxing basically saved John's life. He got control of his body, his emotions, his anger; it was the first time it was all harnessed. It focused him in a direction; it gave him a goal. Boxing is full of short and long-term goals, which you build on every day.

Pre-boxing, John's body was strong but undisciplined. He had some power, but then he learned about running and nutrition and what was good for you and what was bad. Before that, it was just there.

I knew what John meant about the body just being there.

12

making contact and collective rage

Don't report me, but I've yet to see *Schindler's List*. I have been making my way through somber documentaries about life in the shtetls, life in the Warsaw ghetto, immigration stories that included amazing tales of Jewish sheepherder cowboys who settled in the West, including Levi Strauss and his invention of blue jeans. Levi Strauss brought many enticing goods with him on the voyage from Germany, but he gave most of them away, and was left with only canvas. Workers were intrigued by these durable pants he was creating, and when a riveter approached him with a plan to make them even longer-lasting, the American blue jean was born.

Wherever they went, the Jews were trying to fit in and yet remain themselves; it was a constant struggle.

"Honey, come in and watch *A Yiddish World Remembered* with me. After that we can see *The Partisans of Vilna*," I called out to Scott, who was in his study preparing a radio show.

"What is this, a scene out of a Woody Allen movie?" Scott joked. "You know, where he takes her yet again to see six hours of *The Sorrow and the Pity*?"

"Right, and he won't go in because she was late and they missed the credits. It's okay, you don't have to watch with me."

Halfway into the scenes of the shtetl life, I began to wonder about my mother. Had she been in a town or on a farm? There was only one story that I was told. Cereal was left on a windowsill to cool, and my mother, as a little girl, dipped her finger in to taste it and a pig grabbed her hand and she was dragged through the yard. Why would there be a pig? Pigs weren't kosher. Mikki remembers Grandma saying she worked as a maid for a rich lady. Could that have been in the town or where the pig was?

Many years later, when my mother raised her hand to apply lipstick or light a cigarette, I could see the scar from the insistent little teeth of that pig. *She was pulled by a pig*. How could that be part of my lineage?

I watched in the film as the little boys were carried, barefoot in the freezing cold, to the unheated *cheder* (synagogue school) to study twelve hours a day, carrying a candle home to light the way. There was a ceremony—once a boy was toilet-trained, he was given letters of the alphabet to eat, dipped in honey, to symbolize the imbibing of knowledge. Knowledge so precious you swallowed it! *A—my name is Alice.*

I saw the strange little lopsided buildings, many without windows, shacks, barns, dirt-covered streets. The poverty was astonishing. A woman holds her baby in a potato sack fashioned as a carrier. It is full of holes. Such a baby might know only the taste of potatoes in her young life. Yet even the poor had a place of honor in their modest homes, a shelf. *For books.* The reverence for learning gave me chills. In one way or another I'd been studying, reading, all my life. As a teenager, I rearranged the books in my bedroom endlessly. Each title signaled a point in my development, a piece of wisdom, a series of unanswered questions, unforgettable characters. My father revered books. One of his rages was provoked because one of us had written in ink in the *Encyclopaedia Brittanica*. "*Never write in books!*" he bellowed. "*Respect them.*"

And the poor placed a strong value on charity. Shabbas dinner was not complete without feeding someone less fortunate. And the singing and laughter went on despite the hardship. Your name was given you because of your work or your physical characteristics—Beryl Hunchback, Zelig Tailor, Schoyma the Giant, Blind Yankel. I could imagine them depicted in medieval paintings or children's fables.

Jews were everyone's scapegoats, chased out of countries. My mother's shtetl was called Ciechanowicz, one of the oldest shtetls and highly prized as a religious center. Somehow the notion that the Jews were involved in the czar's assassination led to an invasion by the Cossacks, and subsequent raping, looting, maiming, and murder occurred. In 1915, the town was burned to the ground in the pogroms. Mikki, who as a child understood some Yiddish, remembers being four years old and hearing about pogroms from our grandmother, but didn't retain any details. We'll never know exactly what they witnessed and what they narrowly escaped.

Ciechanow, north of Warsaw, is the town mentioned in the ship's roster, and it is likely that this is what my family always called Ciechanowicz. Descendants of this shtetl describe Ciechanow residents as leading impoverished and miserable lives. To get water, there was a specially designated man who walked from house to house with pails from the river and sold it. Each family accumulated the water into a barrel kept in the kitchen for both drinking and washing dishes (unsterilized of course). There was no electricity and no gas, just wood for the oven.

Pride. Pride had been missing from my life. *Ethnic pride*, the kind the boxers wore like a flag when they stepped into the ring. Two women, survivors of shtetls, look out at me from the screen. They are sisters—warm, wise, complex. They begin to sing: It sounds like "shane vid die le voner, lich dich veer de steren," and the tears are out of my eyes before I realize: *That's a lullaby my mother sung to me.* The sing-song tune, the wordless melodies, yoy boy boy boy . . . I remembered more than I thought. The camera passes over an ancient cemetery. Plain as day on one of the stones is a carving of the Vulcan salute from *Star Trek* (a show I'd always loved), a palm raised with two fingers pressed on one side, a space, and two fingers pressed together on the other. I hurried to the

Internet to find an explanation. When he was eight, Leonard Nimoy peeked at a special blessing ceremony in an orthodox synagogue, where designated members of the Kohanim, the genealogical descendants of the Jewish priests who served in he Jerusalem Temple, were holding out their arms and fingers to form the shape of the Hebrew letter "shin" which begins the blessing "Shaddai" (Almighty God).

Years later, when Nimoy participated in the crafting of the half-human, half-Vulcan character Spock, he said that Spock was "a diaspora character if there ever was one." He never really fit in anywhere. With this shaping of a hand, generations of *Star Trek* fans have recognized one another. *Live long and prosper.*

The next morning John and I are training. I grimace and stiffen. John has whacked both my arms near the elbows with the punch mitts. Suddenly these tools, which had been devices for my learning, are weapons. Ow! It smarts. Jab, one-two, he calls out; it's become a familiar mantra. And now, "Cover, cover," meaning I'm coming at you, protect yourself. I quickly get used to the smacks, and it's surprisingly not all that painful and, for some inexplicable reason, I like it. It feels real, it feels like contact; we are even closer now to really boxing. I can be smacked, touched, hit, tapped, poked, jostled. My brain is busy. I have to focus on keeping my legs in a proper boxing stance, open, right leg way back, knees bent. I have to keep my gloves up by my face. *Protect yourself at all times.* I have to constantly watch John's movements. Where is he going next?

"I'm coming at you," he warns. "Slip to the left."

I slip to my right instead and he narrowly misses my head with his mitt. Sometimes I think I'm cognitively impaired.

"That would have hurt. But only for a minute."

"Damnit! Why can't I . . ."

"C'mon, I'm coming at you. Slip to the left, the left."

I try again, thrusting my head toward the left, and now I've got it.

"Do it again! Quick!" I yell.

"I'm coming at you. Slip to the left."

"Again!" I can freely shout out these demands and they will be heard and met.

I slip to the left. Repetition helps.

"You're a kinetic learner," John observes. "You've got to feel it to get it. You can't just have it told to you. Take a break now."

I rest, and the minute passes too fast.

"Do you need more time?" John asks.

"No, I'm fine," I say, lying.

"Okay, now listen, we're going to work that right-hand combo—I need you to roll that shoulder. Double jab, roll, oh oh! that's it . . . Don't dip down, you don't need to dip down, yea! Roll right over—there you go!"

"Wait," I pant, "so is that how I usually move when I slip or am I adding something?

"Well, you're adding a little bit—a little bit more emphasis with the shoulder. When I teach it in the beginning it's just side to side; now it's . . . meaningful."

Meaningful. It sounds dignified and serious. Like it's going to have a significant application at some point.

"Okay, go! Slip! Nice! Again! Slip! There you go, baby! Go! Slip! Elbow up on the hook—remember, if I counter again with my right hand and your elbow's not up, you're wide open . . . Let's do it, kid. There we go! Ha-ha! Now we're talking."

I emit a strange shriek of pride and delight; it's a sound I've never heard come out of my mouth before.

We both laugh now. He gets it.

"There you go, you evil vixen! Good! Uppercut after it. Tight, bang bang. Nice."

Hup. Smack. I'm grunting and punching.

"C'mon c'mon, three more, baby, c'mon."

Snap snap.

"Two more!"

Snap snap.

"Last one! Move!"

And I smack my left hook like I'm exiting a burning building, with fury, force, conviction. All of a sudden there are images in my head, of other people, hurt and starving people, vulnerable, imprisoned people. I'm fighting for them. I let the images morph and gain power—now it's clearly concentration camp victims who have entered my brain in the midst of punching and moving. It's never happened before. Nazis. I'm angry at Nazis. I hate them and want to kill them. I'm punching for more people than just myself, people who have been victimized and tortured.

"What happened there?" John asked.

"Why?"

"You were suddenly so . . . strong."

"I'll tell you," I said, gasping for breath. "I had these images suddenly." I described them to John.

"You accessed some collective rage."

It was like I had taken a psychedelic drug and John was my guide. He'd been there.

"Collective rage," I sigh. "Is that weird?"

"God, no. Do it again. Whatever it takes."

In her fascinating book *Stars of David: Prominent Jews Talk About Being Jewish*, Abigail Pogrebin asks Steven Spielberg about growing up Jewish. He says that in his last year in high school in northern California, he was "slugged in the mouth for being a Jew." He was also kicked in the groin. Boys threw pennies at him in study hall and knocked him into walls. He admits to "fantasizing about getting all these guys in group therapy with me . . . I just wanted to ask them, 'Why did you make my life miserable?'"

Gene Wilder describes being sent to a military academy at the age of thirteen while his mother was ill. As the only Jew there, he was beaten and insulted at every turn. The boys hit his arms black and blue, avoiding his face so no one would know. Finally his mother spotted the bruises while he was changing for dinner one night at home and pulled him out of the school.

Former mayor of New York Ed Koch's problems began when

he was drafted into the army. A guy challenged him, calling him a "Yid." Koch decided not to take it, but he knew he wasn't strong enough at that point to do anything. "I'm going to build myself up and ultimately I'm going to challenge him," he vowed. He still got beat up, but he was very proud of himself for trying, "for the mere fact that I challenged him."

Director Mike Nichols remembers his own arrival at New York City's shores at the age of seven, after escaping from Nazi Berlin in 1939, along with his four-year-old brother. He only knew how to say "I don't speak English."

In *Chutzpah*, lawyer Alan M. Dershowitz recounts chilling examples of anti-Semitism, even as late as 1968. He and his family were excluded from a resort town, Point of Woods, on New York's Fire Island. Some vacation resorts openly proclaimed, "No dogs, no Jews." Coney Island was "restricted." Employment ads stated "Christians only need apply." Many times, homes were sold with instructions not to be resold to "Hebrews."

Pogrebin herself had been ambivalent about what it meant to call herself a Jew, and found in her interviews that many Jews were not very observant. They subscribed to what some call a "smorgasbord" style of Judaism—picking and choosing a holiday here, a practice here, to observe when they felt like it. Others, like Jason Alexander, drew the line at Jews having Christmas trees, and *Kaddish* author Leon Wieseltier states unequivocally that most American Jews have become slackers who are ignorant about their religion. He has no patience for them whatsoever. Yet many whom he would criticize described feeling a deep and unarticulated connection to being Jewish.

I had been unforgivably cruel in my mind as a child. My own relatives had been part of the "stream of penniless Jews who came to America . . . with their pockets empty and their heads full of dreams," but, unlike Budd Schulberg, who described it that way with empathy and respect, I was frightened by their pasts, and nothing deadens curiosity more effectively than anxiety and fear. The "Old Country" was dirt and poverty to me, but since boxing, and reading about the Jewish boxers, every detail was taking on a new life. Each piece was from a richly textured fabric, thick, jewel-encrusted, and precious. I wished I'd been able to get more information from my parents when they were alive. Leon Wieseltier said, "Sooner or later you will cherish something so much that you will seek to preserve it."

My maternal grandfather Isadore, like many of the men, came to America first, promising to send for the family. But he didn't send for my grandmother right away, and there was talk that he found another woman. This was a common phenomenon; the men would come, get taken up with American ways, and not want to send for the shtetl woman so quickly. The National Desertion Bureau was created to deal with the problem. This dilemma is portrayed beautifully in Joan Micklin Silver's film *Hester Street.* The betrayed woman could not get a divorce unless it was an official religious one, in which both parties had to be present with the rabbi, so attempts were made to find the man, who often did not want to be found.

My grandfather joined the army and fought in World War I. My sister Susan was able to attain a scholarship to the University of Chicago for descendants of World War I veterans, a detail I discovered only recently.

My mother, eight years old, dragged along on an ocean trip to a strange, new place, speaking only Yiddish. Her mother, my grandmother, frightened, religious, unsure how or where they would observe. I moved many times in my early twenties, from New Jersey to the Upper West Side of Manhattan, working my way down from 110th Street to 86th, each move improving my neighborhood and circumstances, and then ultimately to several places in Connecticut, where I settled. But I had been able to explore the new neighborhoods, choose them carefully, check out different places. Was there a movie theater nearby? A good bookstore?

My mother, eight years old, on an enormous ship, strange and unimaginable. My grandmother, hoping she would find peace and prosperity in this melting pot country—what could they have been feeling?

❖

There was a day John came in and I could tell he was a little down. "You're in a bad mood, aren't you?" "Wow, you're good," he said. To me it was obvious, but maybe people didn't tend to notice the subtleties of John's moods—they were more intent on what he could give them on any given day. He told me he was "burying Willie Pepp today" and complained of assorted obligations that were making him feel overwhelmed and swamped—a class conflicted with the wake (John was finishing a degree in history), needing to be at the new gym, overdue bills. I remembered that Willie Pepp was a featherweight champion who fought in the tradition of Benny Leonard and who gave John some valuable advice when John was a troubled kid.

I was enjoying the fact that John was sharing his concerns with me, when I suddenly noticed he was pulling a second pair of gloves out of the mesh bag. He began to put them on.

"What's going on—I mean, is this . . . am I . . ." My head was spinning; I'd never seen him in boxing gloves. John had happily relieved other men of their consciousness. What was going to happen?

"I just want you to get used to something coming at you. Here, we'll play like kittens, gentle."

We proceeded to trade punches, of a sort. "Don't worry," he says, "I won't hurt you, don't move back, keep me in front of you." I try to match his rhythm, and when I catch the beat, I am more fluid and responsive; we are in sync and it feels more intuitive and primal. Overthinking—that's the enemy. In high school, fueled by antiauthoritarian hormones of the 1960s, I turned down an invitation to join the National Honor Society. I told Mrs. Baumgartner, my French teacher, that it was elitist and not much of an honor.

"Binnie," she said, her voice dripping with condescension, "you've been reading too many books."

John hadn't been a particularly good student. He considered himself smart but lazy. His report cards consistently stated: "fails to live up to potential." He was interested in writing and reading Mark Twain, and all the Hardy Boys books. In sixth grade he discovered Mickey Spillane and got in trouble for bringing it to school. The teachers said it was seedy, and sent letters home.

❖

Hitting leather punch mitts brings a loud *thwack!* There is a feeling of destiny, of action coming to a halt, of force finding its wall, of a question delighting in its answer. Glove to glove is a crapshoot, an unheard whisper, a snippet of a melody looking for accompaniment.

What will glove to glove be? Or John's glove to my body and head?

"I'm coming at you," John warns. "Catch my punch, and push it away, real easy, almost with a sense of disdain, like get this out of here, just push it down, don't use too much force, don't overdo it, it's just in your way."

There we are, the children of unhappy traveling salesmen and impaired mothers, pounding away at each other.

At the end, I beg for another round—"You addict, you," he said, and we did another round.

Soon after the playing-like-kittens day, John tells me to come to an amateur fight. It's a Saturday night and I'm scheduled to do a four-hour radio show. I arrange to have another DJ fill in for my last two hours, so I can get to this fight. I'm going alone—I asked Scott, but he's clearly got zero interest in watching live boxing and there's no reason to subject him to it. Kristin, who at least has expressed some interest in my boxing, is visiting family in Maine. There's no else to ask.

I hear myself announce this on the air. "I'm going to the fights."

I prop the Mapquest directions on the dashboard and negotiate the highway and back roads of Meriden to find the Vocational High School where they are holding the fight. It's packed. John had put my name on the guest list, so I have no problems getting in. I walk into an enormous gymnasium set up for the boxing match. It's well under way. There is a large ring in the center, and folding chairs packed all around. There are also bleachers on all the sides of the room. The bright fluorescent lights are blazing, and the room is hot and loud. As I walk in, I see John, looking splendid in a tuxedo, in the middle of the ring. He is the ring announcer for the evening, and is holding a microphone. My timing is great; it is between bouts and John quickly spots me, strides over, takes my hand, and walks me over to a row of seats where his people are. I feel all eyes on me; it's a kick.

There I meet two of John's kids, Kelly (fourteen) and Hunter (twelve), and John's girlfriend Stacey. She is there with her two little girls, who are very sweet. In fact, as I look around I see that the room is absolutely filled with kids, who are running around freely in their own little utopia and having fun. I begin to see just how much John is a man with a small dynasty—children, girlfriends, ex-wives, ex-girlfriends, clients. How does he take care of so many people?

My boxing sibling Jenni pops into the seat next to me, looking fit in her jeans and boots, her ever-present cross grazing a low-cut crocheted top, and we embrace. Her kids are here, too. "No bar punches! Stop holding!" she shouts out during the matches. John has taught her well.

I watch the fights intently, on the edge of my seat, enjoying seeing people actually boxing right in front of me, enjoying the DJ's mix of loud music between rounds, and the energy of the room. People are clearly here to have a good time. It's certainly not the image from 1940s and 1950s movies of a smoky room, men screaming for blood, women dressed in coats with huge fur collars and teetering on high heels, wincing when the sweat or blood flies from the ring onto their tightly coiffed heads. This boxing match is a family event.

It is hard, though, to see what is happening in the ring; it's all going so fast. I can't tell what punches are being thrown and what defensive maneuvers are being used. I try to focus on one fighter at a time to watch, then switch off.

During breaks between bouts, instead of scantily clad girls walking through the ring holding up cards identifying the round, there are mostly black or Latino children, proudly displaying a card advertising some local family insurance company or bodega.

Tonight's card features a visiting Marine boxing club fighting the local boys from Silver City boxing gym. The Marines' support for each other is moving, as they shout out instructions from the sidelines, "*C'mon, Martinez, he's getting tired! Keep it up! One-two, one-two! Finish him now!*"

This is amateur boxing, so everyone is wearing protective headgear.

And even a pair of boys, probably eleven years old, 75 pounds each, are on the fight card. They fight like pros. Their trainers, sweat dripping profusely, excitedly urge the little gladiators on, with all the pleasure of gratified parents at a soccer game. "*C'mon son, c'mon son! Jab! That's it! You can do it!*" The boy who loses wears the saddest face in the world.

When John isn't announcing in the ring, he is working the crowd, embracing people, smiling, stopping to chat, checking in with his kids and Stacey. Sometimes he sits in a free chair behind us and checks his notes. Toward the end of the evening, he says, within obvious earshot of everyone, including his kids, "So, Binnie, now I've taken your boxing virginity" (referring to my attending an actual fight).

"Yeah, it only hurt a little," I say, blushing.

"I told you I'd be gentle," John says and leaps back inside the ring to announce the next bout.

When I get home that night, I download the pictures I snapped, and put one of a little boy boxing up as a screensaver. Every day I can see his determined little frame, his fighting stance, and the cheering crowd.

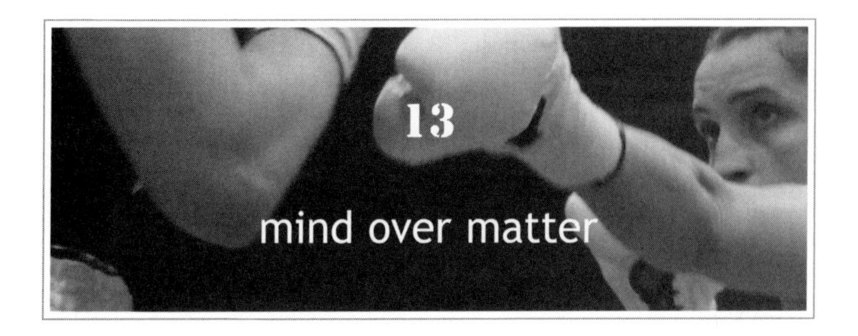

13
mind over matter

Meriden, Connecticut, is a blue-collar town with around sixty thousand people. It's considered the midpoint of Connecticut and to me it's always been lacking in character, a little seedy and depressing. I spent a few hours once doing jury duty there and was mercifully excused from participation in a trial. The storefronts across from the courthouse where one might have lunch were largely empty.

A few months after the fight at the Vocational High School, I was heading back to Meriden to work with John in an actual boxing ring at Beat the Street Community Center, formerly known as Silver City Boxing. Larry Pelletier, who won the first state championship in 1980 at the age of sixteen, runs this six-thousand-square-foot gym and fitness center. He's a man with a mission: to help inner-city kids develop confidence, structure, mental toughness, and discipline through boxing skills.

John suggested I meet him in the parking lot of Dempsey's Bar. That's where he lives, in an apartment above the bar. It couldn't have a better name. It's a rough neighborhood, not the worst in

New Haven surely, but there are often groups of tough-looking guys hanging around on the corner in front of dilapidated buildings. You'll see a brief flame and wonder if they're lighting cigarettes or joints.

"I'm here, parked by the dumpster," I say to John on my cellphone.

"Lemme put my shoes on—be right down." He comes down the three back flights that look like a fire escape.

We transfer my gym bag and purse to his SUV, the Bravada (those marketers know their target), and I get in the front seat, moving aside appointment books, sunglass cases, pens, napkins, and empty Diet Coke cans.

"We're gonna pick up the little ones," John says, already deep into cellphone business as he tells me this. John lives on his cellphone; he's always organizing something with someone, arranging a boxing lesson, reassuring his girlfriend, or talking to his dad.

Aw, so we're not going to the candy store, just you and me? Kid, adult, kid, adult. I think boxing for me may be about trying to decide which one I am.

On the ride to Meriden, I'm awash in the Spehar family culture. Teasing, riffs, colorful language, general silliness, and good humor with Hunter and Kelly.

"There's the old club," John says, pointing to an empty storefront alongside the railroad tracks.

The new club's location is not much better. It abuts a deserted building that has broken chunks missing, like Berlin during wartime. Across the street are a few houses, and people are sitting on their stoops, just as we did in Newark. Stoop culture was a world unto itself, the little zone outside your house that wasn't inside, but wasn't too far outside either.

We go up a staircase to the second floor of this warehouse building, passing 8 × 10 boxing posters on the wall, slapped up with Scotch tape. Once inside the gym, I see a huge flurry of activity. Dozens of young girls, mostly Hispanic, are dancing in front of a mirror, thrusting their little bodies provocatively to the rhythm of the music coming from a boombox on the floor. They are absolutely focused. A few gather on the floor, watching. One is stretched out across an older girl's lap, having her hair braided.

I see two boxing rings on the left, an area with exercise equipment, and some side rooms that look like offices. Half a dozen heavy bags are suspended from the ceiling, pounded on by young bare-chested men wearing bandanas to contain their wild hair. They glance at us. Kelly checks her cellphone and scopes out the guys. Hunter is approached by a former boxer who trains at Beat the Street, who offers to work with him on this night. Hunter's eyes light up, and John looks on approvingly. We're all getting our hands wrapped.

"Age before beauty," I say, sticking my hand out. I don't know how to fit in, but I want to.

"Okay," John says, organizing us. "Hunter's working with Diaz, Kelly, you and Binnie go over to a heavybag and do some rounds while I work a few rounds with Ryan, and then I'll work with the girls."

Ryan had walked in a few minutes ago with his devoted dad. He's John's fifteen-year-old fighter who won his first amateur bout and who John predicts will be headed to the Golden Gloves. Ryan is a delicate-looking young boy with a tiny swatch of hair growing from his chin.

When I watched Ryan fight at an outdoor match, I jumped up and down, shrieking like a groupie, and then watched him get checked out by Samantha Dane, the ringside physican, who likes to be called Sam.

"Who is that?" I asked John when I first saw the red-haired physician taking fighters' blood pressures.

"She's a fighter. And a good one. We worked together. She fought at Gleason's in Brooklyn. She's too good, can't get any more fights. That happens a lot with women—they're too strong and powerful and there aren't other women to match them up with. She's an ER doc—and became a ringside physician because she loves the game."

I'd heard of Gleason's. It was where the new phenomenon of white collar boxing had exploded—attorneys, physicians, executives, all testing themselves in the ring. I was curious about Samantha; she was short, like me, and not young.

Kelly and I pick a bag at the end of the gym, closer to the dancers. I only recently started working the heavybag with John at his gym, and it's a frustrating monster that is all about timing. You try to push it back to get a gentle sway, then punch it when it comes toward you, then stop it with your fist. It sounds simple, but it's not. The bag has tremendous force and a mind of its own, whirling around, and if you catch it at the wrong moment, you feel an unpleasant impact in your arm and shoulder.

Kelly whacks the bag expertly; clearly she's been doing this all her young life. There's a force to her movements, and her upper arms are impressively developed.

"Okay, that's a round," John shouts at us from across the room, signaling that we can take a break. He's been working in the ring with Ryan and he's using oversized punch mitts the size of New Jersey. I've never seen those before. I know I'm going to want my familiar stuff. But *don't ask, don't tell* is particularly important here; we've taken the show on the road and I cannot appear to be a princess.

The little girls are strutting, the music is blasting, the room is unbelievably hot. This must be what Bikram yoga feels like (practiced in a room heated to 105 degrees). I'm sweating fiercely by the second round of bag-punching. Suddenly, a small girl who has been sitting and watching us punching the bags catches my eye and we smile at each other. There's a simple happiness to be found here; certainly more so for me than at a cocktail party.

We are summoned to the ring. Ryan looks wiped out, and I see Hunter in the adjacent ring being given some subtle suggestions about jabbing from Diaz. Everywhere I go in the boxing world, my ears are wide open for tips and techniques I can try out myself. At the edge of the ropes, I am clumsy again, but Kelly shows me how to get into the ring. Jenni once said it was easy for her because one of her foster families had a farm—"It's just like going through a split-rail fence." John calls out commands to

Kelly, then to me: jab, jab jab right, jab, jab jab right, left hook, and so on. We take turns working with him and the giant pads.

"Get over to the ropes," John commands, and proceeds to pummel us with the pads. Then we take turns dropping our left shoulder against his body and push against his elbow with our right glove, getting distance, and throwing a right cross. I enjoy this combination the most. But I'm feeling thirsty, and the water bottle is far away. No one else seems to be needing to drink, despite the incredible heat. Kelly is giggling into her father's face. I decide to take a break for water and go talk to Larry Pelletier, the missionary who runs this amazing place.

Larry is a forty-three-year-old AT&T technician by day, Mother Theresa by night. He has been running this nonprofit club for thirteen years and is absolutely devoted to the kids. I sit on a shabby couch amid yellowing newspapers and boxes of copy paper. Larry takes a call. "Hey, Muhammad, I've got a fighter for your guy, yeah, 215 pounds . . ."

Larry has salt-pepper wavy hair, a mustache, and frameless eyeglasses. He's French/Polish and recently married with a small child. He tells me that boxing is "mind over matter," and that is the lesson he wants to share with kids. It's not about toughness, it's about mental stuff, he says, and they can use that throughout their lives. John often says that a kid who learns to box is going to have very little fear standing up in front of a class giving a book report or less anxiety trying out for the school play.

The building we are sitting in used to be a roller-skating rink, then a duckpin alley, then a dress factory. When Larry was becoming a youth minister at the archdiocese of Hartford, he had a vision of bringing his love of boxing to kids and he's doing it. He did some fighting himself, back in the day, but doesn't miss it. "We've got hip-hop dancing, fitness, a homework class, boxing, pee-wee boxing for four- to nine-year-olds. The class has twenty-five to forty, and the kids just blossom. I'm not in this for the strokes; I'm in it for the kids. We do have dues. If you're over eighteen and you're in school, it's free, but if you're working, like let's say you wanted to work out here, it would be $25 a month."

I could drive up to Meriden to work out in this gym, and have that little girl smile at me again. *I would have to learn to wrap my hands myself.*

"We've got sixty percent Hispanic, then white, black, you name it. My goal is to keep this running and make it a fixture in the community. Some of the kids at Beat the Street Center are often in and out of jail. Right now we're training a young gang member who had gotten shot." The telephone rings again, but he doesn't answer it. He's up on his feet and shuffling through a stack of papers.

"Here, let me show you a picture of the pee-wee group."

I notice that my sweating has finally tapered off, and my hands are steadying, but my eyeballs are still sweating. My eyeballs only started sweating when I started boxing, and it's an odd feeling, hard to describe, but it makes you feel you're involved in something of significance.

Hunter comes in and Larry asks him to give us privacy. Hunter glances at my writing pad. He must wonder who the heck I am and why his father is giving me such total access to their boxing world. I've never seen any deprivation in John's kids, but I am suddenly aware of how hard it must be for them to share their father with the world. And I thought it was hard for me.

"I'm Daddy to a lot of people," John often says.

Larry had mentioned gangs. Johnny Duke, John's trainer, would often intervene in gang warfare. He would get between them in the eleventh hour and bring the two leaders to the table. John as a white kid was an anomaly—the gang members thought he was crazy, or knew what he was doing, or was just heavily armed.

Juvie, gang treaties, cops—it was straight out of *West Side Story*. My sisters and I had seen both the play and the movie, and used to put on the soundtrack and dance around the living room. We knew all the words to all the songs. They accompanied many a long car trip.

Gee, Officer Krupke, we're down on our knees, cause no one loves a fellow with a social disease . . . Tony, Tony . . . Tonight, tonight . . . When you're a Jet you're a Jet all the way from your first cigarette to your last dying day . . . Tony, Tony . . . Tonight, tonight.

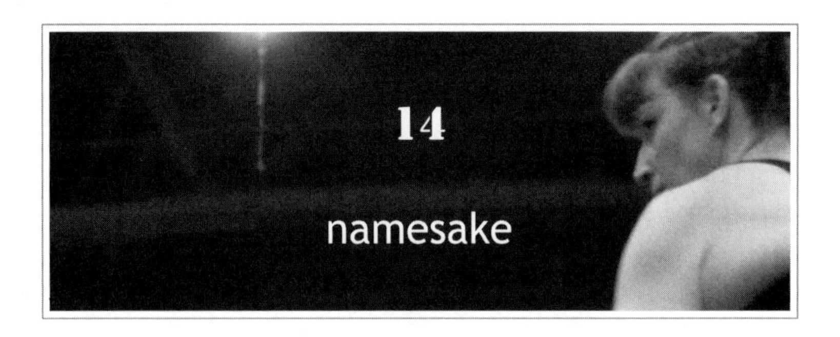

14
namesake

The battles of *West Side Story* were tame compared to the neighborhood brawls on the Lower East Side of New York City in the late 1800s and early 1900s. The best fighters were those who captured the territory, the turf—or had the goods to back up their claim to being the best. The streets were dangerous; if you couldn't defend yourself, you couldn't be out there, and Benny Leonard, being small, was often an object of bullying. Kids fought with anything they could find—baseball bats, rocks, even snowballs packed around chunks of coal.

Benny had a sympathetic uncle who took him to the Silver Heel Club to get some boxing instruction. By eleven years old, Benny was *the* boxer of Eighth Street. He not only liked taking on the bullies, he was mensch enough to protect older Jewish women if they were harassed on their way to synagogue. By the time Benny "The Ghetto Wizard" Leonard was fifteen years old, he had been knocked around in gang wars, illegal fights, and bootleg brawls. Fighters were hungry. Sometimes payment was simply a hot meal, sometimes a few dollars. At first the Irish were in charge of the power structure in the boxing world, and a distinct rivalry was growing between the Jews and the Irish. Benny fought many Irish fighters before he turned professional at just fifteen years old, in 1911, the year my father was born. His mother Minny was fearful that her son would get hurt, like most of the Jewish mothers of fighting sons. He tried to keep his training from his mother, but when the money came in, there was no doubt: he should keep boxing.

Benny was a lightweight, and like most Jewish fighters had a sinewy, muscular body. He was considered a gentlemen, and extremely bright. He fought for humanitarian causes, and a journalist once wrote, "Benny Leonard has done more to conquer anti-Semitism than textbooks." Benny studied fights like a scholar, developing brilliant footwork and clever defensive strategies. He wasn't considered the strongest of fighters, but the blows themselves were precise, fast, and well-timed, and that made all the difference.

When World War I broke out, Benny joined the army, like my grandfather Barney. But when Benny returned, he fought everyone, and made a modest fortune, enough to open some businesses. However, he lost everything in the Depression and at thirty-five had to try again to fight to make money.

When I fantasize meeting Benny Leonard, I picture us at the infamous Stillman's Gym, what A. J. Liebling called "The University of Eighth Avenue." I don't know how I get in, because there are no other women there, but that's the beauty of fantasy.

Benny walks me up the stairs and starts telling me about how he first came to Stillman's.

"We were all at Billy Grupp's, that was the gym where everyone trained, up on 116th Street. But one day, Grupp, he was unpredictable, starts talking about Jews in a derogatory way, well, actually, he was also inebriated, but still he implied that we were the cause of World War I. So I took everyone, I mean I led us right out of there. So we wind up at Stillman's storefront, first in Harlem, and then eventually the real one, on Eighth Avenue."

Leonard is not as handsome or devilish as Barney Ross, but he has another head of dark hair that he doesn't like anyone to muss up, and he's got this way about him; you feel like you could listen to him forever.

"Right about here, here's where you'd pay your fifteen cents to the guy with the little glasses, Curley."

I look up at the tall ceiling and then down again to a row of folding chairs where I can imagine guys sitting, cigars firmly tucked in mouths, occasionally spitting on the floor. There are two raised rings, side by side.

"Who was Stillman exactly?" I ask. We sit down on a couple of ancient metal folding chairs.

"Ah, that's kind of a mystery. Some say he was a cop once. One thing I know, he was like a piece of sharp metal, and always yelling. No soft side to that fellow."

The windows look glued shut. Narrow, dented, green metal lockers line the walls.

George Plimpton was a journalist who competed in sports to learn about the games, and boxing was one of them. He was the inventor of "immersion journalism." Although Plimpton's trainer begged him to stay out of Stillman's because he'd probably get some awful disease, he did go there to prepare for his brief experience boxing and described it this way:

> A dark stairway led up into a gloomy vaultlike room, rather like the hold of an old galleon. One heard the sound before one's eyes acclimatized: the *slap-slap* of the ropes being skipped, the thud of leather into the big heavy bags that squeaked from their chains as they swung, the rattle of the speed bags, the muffled sounds of gym shoes on the canvas (there were two rings), the snuffle of the fighters breathing through their noses, and, every three minutes, the sharp clang of the ring bell. The atmosphere was a fetid jungle twilight.

In other words, Stillman's was a total dump. The great Angelo Dundee, Muhammad Ali's trainer, said the windows in the place were "a monument to dirt and grit, never opened and so caked with layer upon layer of filth that even the pigeons had given up trying to look in." Gene Tunney, the bookish boxer who never quite won the public's love, said he could not believe the stench: "Let's clear this place out with some fresh air," he said. Johnny Dundee, the featherweight champion, reportedly replied, "Fresh air? Why, that stuff is likely to kill us!"

"But just two blocks from the Garden, what could be more perfect?" Benny asks rhetorically.

"After sparring, we'd all go down to the bar, the Neutral Corner," Benny goes on. "Eighth Avenue also had the Ringside Bar. But the Neutral Corner was sweet. You'd find everybody who was anybody there, in the afternoon, siesta time, 3 to 5 p.m. Stillman's was closed during those hours, so you could get a ten-cent beer and listen to the stories."

"Mr. Leonard, I think you met my friend Steve Acunto there once?" I say.

"Ah, let me see. Small fellow? Wiry? Lightweight? Yes, I recall. I walked into Stillman's and there he was in the ring. Lou Ambers, great lightweight, real solid jab, was working with him. And I walked right up and said, 'Kid, who taught you that style?' Because he was boxing like me! And the kid says, 'I've been watching all the films of your fights!' So I brought him downstairs to Riker's for a cup of tea and he looked up to me, you know, I was the older fellow, so I held forth for a while and he drank it in. I said it was a rough sport, but there was also a science to it, and that's the truth. Boxing taught me more than any university. It made a real man out of me. If I had a child and he wished to learn about boxing, I wouldn't hesitate to introduce him to the finer points. It gave me my life."

I look around at the two rings in front of us, and imagine all the great fighters that had worked their asses off in them.

"Do . . . you have any questions?" Benny Leonard asks me.

"Yes. I do. There is something. I don't feel that strong. I mean I feel powerful, but I don't know if I can ever get my arms to be as strong as a man's, or other women who are just stronger. Maybe it's genetic. I don't know. I use the weight machines, but I don't know if my right cross is ever going to get more powerful," I say.

"Listen, my portion of knockouts is not that impressive. The truth is, I wasn't so strong myself. But I never made the same mistake twice. I watched everything. I kept my head sharp. Size up your opponent, develop a strategy, and you'll do fine. Accuracy, accuracy, and never give up. Someone once said, 'To rest is to rust.' Does that help?" Leonard looks at me.

"It will. Just to get a few words from you—I can't believe it. I read that in the *Jewish Daily* bulletin they said you were greater than Einstein."

"Aw, how can that be?" Leonard stares at his shoes.

"Well, the way they figured it, Einstein was known at first in America by only thousands, but millions knew you."

"The Jewish papers," Leonard says. "They didn't know much about prizefighting, but I guess they appreciated its popularity."

The stale air in Stillman's is getting to me, so I say goodbye to Benny Leonard, of whom boxing historian Bert Randolph Sugar, known for his incisive wit, ever-present cigar and fedora, said, "Benny Leonard was like an artichoke—the more you peeled away the more you discovered. Leonard was the nearest thing to a perfect fighter boxing has ever seen."

In 1947, the same year my sister Susan was born, Benny was working as a referee in St. Nick's arena in Manhattan. He staggered and fell. At fifty-one, he died of coronary thrombosis.

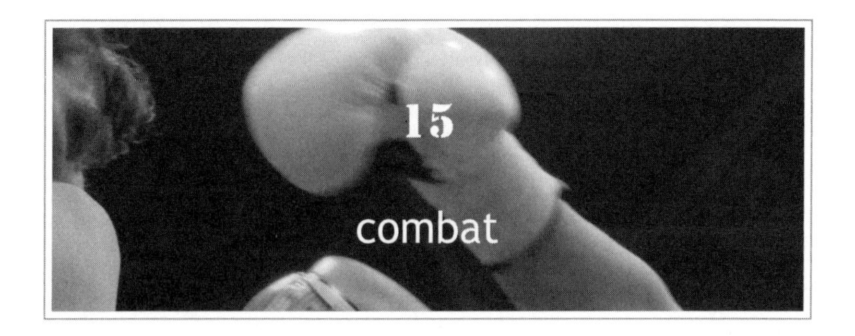

I now own my own boxing gloves, read *Ring* magazine, and watch fights on television any chance I can. I can no longer complain when Scott is glued to the Red Sox games—chances are while he's in the bedroom watching baseball, I'm in the living room watching men pound each other on the other television. Sometimes he'll walk into my room and we just look at each other and laugh.

On weeks when I didn't get to box, I felt restless and irritable. I loved my new red gloves, and I was considering monogramming them because they basically looked like everyone else's. I didn't know if that would be considered tacky or cool. We worked with the gloves regularly now. John wanted them to mold to my hands. But halfway through my workouts, my right forefinger and thumb felt numb. We'd take off the gloves, rewrap, readjust, but kept running into the same problem. Until one day John took them home. "Let me wear them for a while and work them in."

I never had the numbness again, and felt that my gloves had been anointed and strengthened by his wearing them.

Having my own gloves meant I needed a bag to transport my stuff. I was now schlepping gloves, handwraps (my own, also), water bottles, deodorant, change of clothes, and Tums (boxing sometimes gave me acid indigestion). A little snack of stuffed cabbage and it might as well have been "Bubbie Goes Boxing." I kept my bag inside a wicker chest in my kitchen, where I also keep birdseed and dog towels. One day the birdseed must have spilled and, when I took out my gloves at the gym, tiny thistle seeds came pouring out. John vacuumed up this little domestic mess, despite my offers to do it.

Pictures of Laili Ali, Lucia Ryker, and Muhammad Ali were now lining my study walls at home. I walked around the house shadowboxing. I went to a health club nearby for steam and sauna, used the treadmill, and lifted weights on nonboxing days. I was feeling stronger and more fit. On walks in the woods, I was no longer having trouble matching my stride with Scott's long legs. My silhouette still loomed large in the mirror, but I could look at it with admiration.

Then came a momentous day. No forewarning, no clues, no signs.

I'm at the gym and John and I have been doing rounds with punch mitts. We constantly experiment with our CD musical accompaniment. We hate limp folk-rock that the other trainers sometimes leave on. "Music to get stoned by," John calls it. We don't like abrasive heavy metal either. Moby is the best. We like to be pumped-up by driving percussion. During a break, I flip through the CDs and when I turn around John is bending down and reaching into another mesh bag.

Out comes protective headgear.

Oh my god. I'm not ready. I can't do it. I can't do the backward somersault. Maybe next time. Maybe I'll just be like Sue, who likes the mitts and doesn't need to spar.

"John?" I squeak.

"It's okay, baby."

"John, wait . . . wait."

"No, it's time."

He walks right up to me, holding a menacing black leather helmet. He gently moves my hair back behind my ears and places the helmet onto my head. I'm being crowned, but in a dark and claustrophobic way. He starts tightening the strap at the neck. My head is now outlined in black, cheeks protected, nose and mouth poking through. I steal a glance in the mirror. It's not attractive. I look like a chubby devotee of S&M.

John puts on headgear, too, and adjusts his strap in front of the mirror.

We stand facing each other.

"John, I have to tell you something."

He waits, silently.

"Okay, I didn't want to tell you before, because I didn't want you to treat me any differently, you know, like with kid gloves, ha-ha, but I . . . I have a collapsed disc in my neck. At C5. You know, it's degenerative arthritis or something, and . . ." I'm practically hyperventilating. *I have my period. Just let me go out in the rowboat.*

"I'm not going to hurt you."

"Okay."

"I will never use my right hand on you, never."

And then, suddenly, I am reassured, and it becomes a nonissue. And I've come out of the closet with one of my secret infirmities, and John is quite nonplussed. He's probably heard much, much worse. After all, since a lot of his clients are middle-aged women, there must be plenty of tales of bad knees, back trouble, hypertension, god knows what. Or maybe we're all just hiding out, pretending to be butch?

I think I am desperately afraid John will remove our gear, sit me down, and say, "It's been fun, but we can't proceed. Too risky."

"Okay, it will take you a while to get used to having this on your head."

"Yeah, like for one thing, I feel like I can't see."

"You can. What we're gonna do is, I just want you to get used to it—so, you know, throw a jab. Go on! Jab!"

I throw my jab, by now a sense-memory punch I've done it so many times. But I don't know where to land it. There's no punch mitt! So I throw vaguely in John's direction.

"You mean . . . at your . . . face?"

He laughs.

"Yes, at my face, silly! Okay, jab!"

This time I bring my left hand out in front of me and throw it higher and more in the middle. The punch mitt was always out to the side. I look at John's eyes, his nose, and push forward. He slips expertly. I've hit nothing.

"Again, again! Jab, jab one-two!"

Flailing, I push my jab forward, then my right, over and over as we move in circles.

I am out of breath much more quickly. I am also overwhelmed by the fact that John is not only asking me to hit him, he is reaching out and hitting *me*. I feel the impact, it's never very strong, but I'm definitely being buffeted by something coming at me. John. John is coming at me. I have to be careful now. The stakes are higher. I'm trying to remember everything he ever said—protect yourself at all times, keep your hands up, cover your face, keep your right leg back, don't drop your hands, snap back the jab, keep your composure. Breathe.

"Keep jabbing! See what's out there!"

"What do you mean? See what's out there?" I gasp.

"See where I am. Find your range."

Range? It's all meaningless. I can't get at him, whether I'm far back or close up.

I find myself up against his body, trying to pound him gracelessly on his middle. I want to just lean onto him and collapse. I can understand now why referees often shout, "No holding!" The fighters are basically embracing each other to grab a moment's rest.

"No! Too close, get back!"

As soon as he stops speaking, I'm fending off another blow. Our work has never been as fast, as complicated, and I have never felt so incompetent.

Bop! He hits me on the side of my head. Whoosh! Arms are moving past me. I look at his body. He's moving from side to side like a beast of prey, sizing me up, predatorial. I try to mimic his moves, and feel idiotic. I just want to make contact. The frustration is enormous. He's quick.

"Jab! Use the two-second rule! Don't let more than two seconds go by without a jab. Keep trying. It doesn't matter if your punches don't land. Every fighter throws more punches than he can land."

Clang! I've been reprieved by the bell, the blessed bell.

"How do you feel?" John asks.

"Good! I mean awful, tired, but good!" We sit down for a minute on the giant exercise balls, which make great seats. I am fully disoriented. I'd never expected to do anything like this. I don't know what to think or feel. I am just completely inside the experience, determined to stay with it, however it feels. I remember reading a book called *Flow*, about a state in which one is so completely involved and engaged there is almost a loss of self.

Clang! My reprieve ends. I leap up, move toward John. During the break I was thinking about a move I could try. What if I pulled back a little, pretending I was going to jab, and then threw a right? A feint.

"Here we go! See what's out there!" John is batting me about.

I jab several times. It's familiar and reliable. I'm thinking about my feint. When can I try it? How can I put it all together onto this constantly moving target? Suddenly I'm ready, and I jerk forward a bit as if to jab with my left and then bam! I've thrown my right and hit John right on his nose, right in the middle of his face.

"Good! That's it, baby, nice. You faked me out."

Giddy with my success, I start flailing and try for a left hook on the side of his head. He ducks. I've almost spun myself around in the process.

"Never turn your back. Never. Or you'll wake up in the locker room."

I'm dazzled. I hit this man. I have made contact. It feels amazing.

Clang! After several more rounds, John removes my headgear. I am dripping with sweat. We embrace, and I'm crying.

"I am very, very proud of you," he says, looking intently into my eyes. "You are now part of an elite group that has faced this thing most people will never face. And you did very well."

There is a special place in the world for people who are tough. Watching two people demonstrate this physical and mental toughness strikes at a deep place inside us. It calls to the courageous part of us that would stand up to the bully, protect a loved one, fight to the finish if necessary.

My tears are of joy. Words begin tumbling out: "Could we, I mean, I'd love to . . . do you think we could ever . . . have an exhibition . . . and I could invite my family and friends . . . and we could just show a few things?"

"You want me to throw the fight?" John says, half-serious.

"God, no, no one would believe it . . . just make me look good. It would be good for the club, publicity and all, and . . . we could have music, I could organize it . . ."

I'm way ahead of myself (the next day, like a woman who can't remember what's she said during labor, I've forgotten all about the idea). But another one came to me. A Box-Mitzvah. I wanted to have a Box-Mitzvah.

"Baby, I'd do it for you, forget the club. I'd do it just for you."

I pack up and drive down to the Milford Shopping Mall, where I often go after boxing to have a snack, browse at Borders, or occasionally go to a movie. This time I set up my laptop in front of the fireplace at Panera's, eat some lukewarm pumpkin soup, check my email, and within several minutes, I am fast asleep.

A buzzer goes off, signaling that an order is ready, and I awake thinking I've got another round to go. I hope I wasn't snoring. I look around. Panera's has the same comforting color scheme of the Starbucks chain, earth tones, golden pendants, graphic designs on the wall. People pick up their food, empty their trays, refill their sodas. A woman is feeding a baby in a stroller. Men in suits are discussing business, laughing loudly for the middle of the day. A silent couple morosely push food around on their plates.

I know I still look the same, like a pleasant middle-aged woman enjoying a bite to eat, but I have a victory stored deep inside me that no one but John and I know, and I'm going to nurture it and savor it, and it's going to grow.

I can already feeling it growing inside, flexing its fingers and toes like a tiny baby, moving into my future.

16

pain and violent zen

I'd upped my boxing lessons to twice a week when I began to experience significant pain in my right leg. I'd be doing my happy stroll through the mall and my leg would feel heavy, fatigued, achy, and sometimes tingly. Sometimes I'd have to sit down and put my leg up, rest it for five minutes, before I could even continue. Could the now-healed fractures have anything to do with it? I began to worry. Once again, I didn't tell John. I didn't want to complain. In the film of Oliver Sacks's *Awakenings*, Robert DeNiro plays a catatonic patient who is brought out of his decades-long comatose state with the experimental drug L-dopa, welcomed into a whole new and exciting world, and then, tragically, the drug begins to wear off, and he slips away again.

I had found boxing, but would I awaken from this dream and go back to somnolence and sloth? Would boxing begin and end with an injury? In the classic 1954 film *On the Waterfront*, washed-up former prizefighter Terry Malloy's famous speech was always dear to my father's heart: "*You don't understand! I coulda had class. I coulda been a contender. I coulda been somebody, instead of a bum, which is what I am.*"

Once we began the actual sparring, it became a staple of our sessions. I'd drive to the gym imagining possible combinations, what I might try on a given day. Maybe I could get in a blow to the body, maybe I could move around a little more. We'd work the punch mitts for a while, and then the headgear would come out.

My pain may have begun with an innocent comment from John one Monday evening.

"I thought about you over the weekend."

"Oh yeah?" I threw a punch and liked both the sound of my hit and what John said.

"I was thinking about your sparring, and I was trying to figure out why you had trouble getting inside, and how you would lose your balance and get flustered. So I figured it out. It's your stance."

"What?" I asked.

"You're not really in a proper boxing stance—you've got to keep your right leg further back and planted firmly on the ground."

"Like this?" I opened my legs more and stiffened my back leg. Then I began to hit, and a door opened and I was stronger and more fluid. Things like this happened frequently. John would notice a critical detail, I'd make the change, and my boxing would be better. He would tell me to work from my core, he would tell me to tighten up, he would use the word "compact" and I'd picture myself shrinking down into an intense little ball. From then on I kept that back leg stiffer, maybe too stiff.

"Sam asked about you," John was saying.

"Sam Dane? The woman I saw working as the ER doc for the tournament? She did? What did she say?"

"She asked if you were sparring yet."

We sat down and took one of our breaks.

"Ah." I tried to hide my excitement. "And what did you say?"

"Oh, I told her yes, you were." He waited. He seemed mysteriously vague.

"That—I mean that would be so interesting . . . to spar with another woman, more my size." Sam was even shorter than me, much thinner, much more fit. And of course she had actually fought, in the ring, at Gleason's, with other women. And she had won!

"So that's why I put it out there—to see what your reaction would be. I don't think you're ready, though. And she's just so competitive."

"Right, right," I mumbled, already fantasizing about it. "I'm definitely not ready and won't be for a long time. It's just, um, a tantalizing thought . . ."

So how could I get ready?

From then on when I boxed with John I thought of Sam Dane. I pictured her small tight frame and pretended I was her—compact, athletic, strong. I got hold of some videos of her fights, and read an interview. She's a "mosquito"—she moves in and bites you and then moves away.

Later that week I called the "mosquito" and asked if I could take her out to lunch because I was doing some boxing research and was learning to box myself. We met at a Friendly's halfway between our houses and Sam pulled up in a black Honda sportscar with her partner Sheila. The sportscar was like a mosquito, too, as it darted into the lot, zippy and powerful like Sam herself.

I ordered a grilled cheese with tomato, a good staple for basic restaurants, and I watched Sam and Sheila enjoy ice cream sodas. Sam was much smaller than Sheila, who had a more imposing frame, but both had a very quiet and respectful manner.

"So what made you get into boxing?" I asked Sam.

"Well, I was very athletic and played every sport at our small high school in Alaska—volleyball in the fall, basketball in the winter, track all year long. Throughout the years I was in nursing school I played rugby. I puddle-jumped through San Francisco, Sonata Rose, Minnesota, upstate New York. Then I went to medical school at the University of Rochester, then for the infamous "match" of residents and schools I was assigned to the University of Connecticut, where I could specialize in emergency medicine. That's when the boxing began."

"Were your parents athletic?" I asked, picturing mine at their posts in club chairs in the living room.

"Oh yeah—Dad was athletic and my mother was a dancer."

"So in medical school . . ." I wiped some mustard off the corner of my mouth.

"At the gym I met a young amateur fighter there who wanted to go pro. He taught me punches, ab work, push-ups, and overall conditioning. Then when I did my residency in Connecticut I found Wally Islam in East Hartford and actually got into the ring and worked the pads. I had to drop it though, because I was more into rugby."

"I was a tussler as a kid, pretty strong, too. I could pull myself up on ropes with just my arms. I got into tussles with boys. I didn't want to hit girls, though. I had no compunction at all about hitting guys. This was in fifth, sixth grades. I don't know, I probably instigated the fights. One time, someone told my father that I got into a fight on the playground. Well, then my father trained me just as he trained his boys—took me hunting, fishing, hiking. Mom was not into this at all. She worried about me going out camping by myself. In sixth grade, two of us girls snuck off to go camping with two boys out in the woods. I was fiercely independent," Sam said.

"Did you have any physical injuries as a kid?" I asked.

"Let's see, a serious concussion with a loss of consciousness when I was hit by a baseball in fifth or sixth grade. Then I got hit right off the tee by a golf ball in the same year. But there was absolutely no change in my fearlessness about activity. While playing rugby at college, I got some injuries, my rib, hand . . . I couldn't risk those—they interfered with my livelihood as an ER doc, so I started running and doing mountain biking."

"And the boxing . . ."

"It was one of those New England winters, cold and dark. I felt that Sheila and I needed to get physically active." She looked over at her partner and they nodded at each other. "I found this crazy guy doing conditioning classes based on boxing . . . and individual lessons. I dragged Sheila to classes with me. That guy was John, and it was 2000."

"Do people know that you box? What do they think?" I asked.

"At first I didn't tell people at work that I was boxing, what with the negative stigma attached to it. But after a while people noticed that I was more than ready to step into physical altercations in the department, like when someone has to be restrained—I started to get a rep . . . and I liked it."

I loved Sam's frankness; she made no apologies for loving contact sports.

"Eventually John lined up a fight for me at Gleason's in Brooklyn."

"People don't understand boxing," Sheila interjected suddenly, "especially amateur. It's very tactical."

"So I fought Nan Mooney," Sam went on. "Virgin fights for each of us. Nan was thirty-something. It was a party. John and I got lost on the way down. I was nervous to the point of my vision narrowing and I couldn't hear John at all from the corner. He kept yelling, "Get your hands up."

"How'd you do?" I asked. Sam and Sheila again exchanged knowing glances.

"She whipped my butt. She was tall and I couldn't get inside. I'm five foot one on a good day when I'm fresh out of bed. But I had three more fights, all at Gleason's. One was a woman who was going to do Golden Gloves. The two of us just stood in front of each other and beat the crap out of each other.

"I wanted more fights but it became very hard to find opponents, and then there was a transition where John introduced me to jujitsu, so I took a summer off and boxed at a jujitsu studio in Derby and John was in transition with where he was working. He gave me permission to start training with Roger Denton. I'd work out on bags by myself and spar with Roger. Roger comes from mixed martial arts. He's quick and fast.

"I also became a ringside physician. There aren't a lot of docs who want to do amateurs because there is no pay, no publicity—it's not televised. Also, there's no medical backup. In the pros, they have an ambulance standing by."

"What kind of things do you say to the fighters if they've been hit?" I asked.

"I ask them things like: What just happened? What did you get hit with? Do you know where you are? Do you have a headache? Are you nauseous? I try to quickly assess global issues, like how alert and awake are they. If they're still confused, I have to make quick decisions like, can I send them to the locker room, can I get them out of the ring, do I need to send them to the hospital? Maybe one percent or fewer people go to the hospital in these amateur fights."

"When I fight I access free-floating anger . . . I did go after one woman because I was mad at her in a round-robin sparring session—she had done a jujitsu thing with Sheila and was over-aggressive. I got pissed off. I asked for John's permission to put a whupping on her and he said yes and I did."

Sheila laughed.

"I think there's a different way that women express competition and aggression. Women have been taught to shove it down—there is a bubbling pot just waiting to spill over. I call it Violent Zen."

I turned to Sheila. I had seen her referee a fight—she was forceful, dynamic, definitive. The fighters completely respected all her decisions and I asked her if she also boxed.

"Yeah, a little. But it took me forever to even hit John—it's not my nature to hit something. I got hit by John the first time, I realized 'he hit me,' and I got angry and tried to hit back."

I found out that Sheila considered herself a tomboy as a child. There were primarily boys in the neighborhood and she also protected her younger brother. So there was a certain amount of hitting going on.

"I didn't grow up with prohibitions about what a girl could or should do," she said.

Sheila studied engineering at Annapolis, going through the Navy from there. Then she went into the Marine Corps for four years.

I asked Sheila how she got into boxing.

"Sam had to get me out of the house!"

"There is something that remains after you come home, you carry it with you, a certain confidence, along with humility . . .

like I made my body do something I couldn't do before." Sheila said, and they nodded. "I did do one bout at Gleason's, just to do it." They exchanged smiles again.

Something told me not to ask how that fight came out.

"How did you get into being a ref?" I asked. These women were dazzling me with their accomplishments and courage. I gazed at them, a neophyte filled with admiration.

"I was going to events because Sam was the ringside doc, but I didn't like doing nothing."

"I can so relate," I said. "I'm nursing an injury."

"I hate all pain," Sam said, mysteriously.

"So I shadowed a guy," Sheila went on, "and you know we were this boxing couple, two women, kind of unusual, and people wanted us both involved, so pretty quickly I took the test to become an official judge and then the next week they threw me in to be an official ref."

"What makes a good ref?" I'd seen so many different styles while watching fights—the refs who did a lot of disciplining and the refs who seemed more uninvolved.

"First off, it's about the boxer, not about you. You should be in the background. First thing to focus on is the safety of the boxer. Protect the weaker boxer. When we're counting, we're making sure in a nonmedical way if he's okay. If his eyes are fluttering, I'm worried."

"I feel irritable when I don't fight," I blurted out.

"Oh yeah," Sam said. "When I'm not fighting, watch out. Women who get involved in any martial art in middle age are a breed apart."

We all start grabbing for the check, and I make sure to wrest it away from these competitors.

As we're walking out, there's a group of women blocking the aisle, chattering away, some of them pulling out cigarettes to get ready to light outside the restaurant. Sam bumped against one of them accidentally.

"Hey watch it, you!" the woman said to Sam, in a sarcastic tone.

"Well, if you'd just move your fat ass, I could get by."

"What did you just say?" the woman was incensed.

Sheila grabbed Sam by the arm and hustled her out the door. "C'mon, let's go; it's not worth it, let's go."

I could see that Sam was aching to go back.

"I guess we all better start boxing again soon," I said and we all laughed and gave each other hugs.

There we were, three middle-aged practitioners of Violent Zen.

I still want to spar with Sam, I thought, as I got into my car and began vigorously massaging my aching right leg.

17

annie oakley's anxieties

Okay, truth be told, boxing wasn't exactly my first experience with an unusual hobby. I'm a rifle shooter. I was vacationing at a lake house in western Massachusetts. Scott and I had gone there every summer for several years. One year, when I was forty-five, a wiry and grizzled fellow with twinkling eyes appeared at the back door. Our neighbor Henry was an eccentric fellow who lived alone in a makeshift house on the edge of the property, which had belonged to his family for many years. He hunted, built things, was self-sufficient, and not particularly happy with civilization, especially highway traffic. He delighted in showing me close-up photographs he'd taken of the bears who visited his yard. "Don't feed 'em, though," he warned.

"Excuse me, sorry," Henry said. "We're gonna be shooting skeets out back, and I hope you don't mind the noise. And, um, if anybody ever wants to learn about guns, by the way, just let me know!"

"I do!" There it was, the projectile utterance. No one else was interested in learning.

Henry was a local NRA official on a mission. He wasn't a violent guy in any way. He'd probably only use a gun to protect himself or to make sure he could eat in the winter. He wanted people to learn about guns so they could use them safely. "After all," he said, "say a neighbor calls you, and they've just moved into an old house and they go in the attic and there's a rifle there, and they don't know how to make sure about its safety. Well you could go on over and check it out and tell them what to do."

It was an unlikely scenario that appealed to me tremendously.

During the rest of our stay, Henry would often appear at the door and I would follow him down the hill to his little house, where he set up some targets against a pile of logs. He had quite a collection of rifles and pistols. He painstakingly showed me how to hold them, load them, and shoot them. Turned out, I was good at it.

We started with the rifle mounted on a bench. I sat behind it, and he taught me how to hold my breath, make myself still, focus on the target, and gently, ever-so-gently, squeeze the trigger. Over and over we would shoot, ignoring the mosquitoes and the gradually darkening skies. When I did well, Henry would say, "Do it again. Make that same picture." I'd go back to our house jubilant. *Grandfather transference.*

"Ah," Scott would say. "Great."

When we were back in Connecticut I received a letter from Henry. He'd picked up a used Russian target rifle for me for $100 at a gun sale. Did I want to come and get it from him?

I drove up to Goshen and brought turkey sandwiches to Henry's house. We sat amid piles of old *National Geographic* magazines and canned goods and talked about rifles. I gave him the money and asked if he would ever come down to Connecticut and meet me to shoot. He knew a range there called Lyman's, but he didn't like driving on the highway.

Henry never did come, but we did exchange some letters for a while. My friend Kristin bought me a canvas rifle case from L. L. Bean (she liked this hobby—"come the apocalypse you can shoot our food") and I went up to the Lyman Range where I lay on a dusty floor in a cubicle and shot at a paper target clipped many yards away. Then I pulled it back to me, just like in the movies, and started over again. In addition to bench shooting, Henry had taught me to shoot while lying prone, while kneeling, and while standing. I bought a special shooting jacket and stiff workboots.

Local women who all seemed to have gone to the same hair salon sometimes gathered for meetings of the ladies pistol club, and a high school boy training for the Olympics unpacked an expensive rifle case in a cubicle near me. A little boy named Remington wandered around. The vibe was focus, focus, focus. *Make that same picture.*

Shooting was tremendous fun, and I loved improving my scores, but shooting at Lyman's was a lonely enterprise, especially without Henry.

Friends laughed, especially at a photograph of me holding a rifle across my body. "You look like Lee Harvey Oswald," they joked. "And you're a vegetarian!" As if I was going to be hunting caribou. Shooting took a hit, no pun intended, when I was diagnosed with a collapsed disc in my neck. Shortly before my husband and I married in 1999, we purchased an unpretentious ranch house with an above-ground pool in the backyard. It was my permanent motel with a pool. Hysterical with happiness, I swam aggressively around its edges, wearing a flotation vest, and keeping my head so hyper-extended above the water (still unhappy about water in the orifices) that I wound up with neck pain. I went for the X-ray. Another orthopedic practice, a miniature factory of ankles, knees, necks, shoulders.

"Do you know that there's a disc in your neck that is completely collapsed?" The orthopedist, bored because he wouldn't be going in with his knife (I wasn't a good candidate), spit out his words with both a jaded and foreboding tone. The words "completely collapsed" had the whiff of admission to a special school, but one that would only end at the Big Graduation in the Sky. I later learned that many, many people walk around with degenerated or collapsed discs, often asymptomatic, but this was the first brush with my body's degeneration caused by aging. I had probably exacerbated damage that was already there.

Years later we dismantled the pool, leaving a round crevice of burnt grass in the ground deep enough to summon a UFO. It wasn't just my neck problem that led to the pool's demise; Scott found the hours and expense of upkeep with chemicals daunting.

Still, it was hard to give it up.

At least there was the temperate therapy pool at Gaylord. This was my idea—I had heard it was good for arthritic damage. I became fluent in the language of damage and slippage—"I have a totally collapsed disc at C5," I would say confidently, wishing for both sympathy and admiration, adding, "C3 is also a little bit tipped," a detail supplied by a "holistic" chiropractor, who tested muscles and used little vials of toxins to see what was what. C3 was responsible for the headaches, he said, C5 was something you might see in eighty percent of autopsied bodies. Still, I could not move my head smoothly to the right or left, and tried to pretend there wasn't much to see in either direction.

Under the guidance of perpetually helpful physical therapists who joined me in the pool, bedecked in aquatards, I learned to swim on my back wearing two flotation devices, one a cervical collar made in Germany that I ordered on the Internet, and a wide blue flotation belt that has become ubiquitous at aquatics centers. I even began using a snorkel-mask to expand my repertoire of swimming styles. I could then be on my stomach without popping my head out of the water in that foolish repetition I had so enjoyed.

For weeks I swam eight, ten, twelve laps, trying out different collars, even slipping off the belt for a few laps, and marveling at my newfound locomotion, which made me feel like a more finished human being, more substantial. After many productive weeks of treatment at the rehab pool, I went one night for "open swim," where the graduates refine their skills. At the front door sat two people in wheelchairs. The woman had long grey hair, loose and tangled, and the man was very aged and tangled as well. "Could you pick that up for me—I've only got one leg," the woman said, motioning down to a lighter pinned beneath the man's sneaker. That was how they were holding onto it. Happy to be helpful, I retrieved the lighter, noting the empty space under the blanket covering her body. And I swear to god, it came out of my mouth, "Sure, but should you be smoking?" It just flew out. The woman laughed, and she said they were "old-timers," suggesting that they were entitled to all indulgences. I felt a pang—what was I thinking? Here they are, trapped in these chairs, limited in a way I could not imagine, while I fretted about the subtleties of moving through space and time, and I'm questioning their habits?

As I descended to the basement and walked the long halls, I thought of *The Shining.* At night the facility was grim and dark. The aquatherapy class was just finishing up; people were piling up their brightly colored foam noodles beside the pool. One woman was floating in the deep end, tangled up in yellow, pink, and orange, like a neon pretzel. I was thrilled at the thought of having the pool to myself. Two lifeguards chatted quietly in the corner. I strapped on, began the backward journey, and it happened.

A bad thought burst in: What am I really lying on? What is under me? This doesn't feel good. This feels weird. I feel floaty and light, too light. What am I going to do? The familiar edge of panic had touched, and I was in the middle of the pool, in twelve feet of deep water. I looked toward the lifeguards and considered a weak "I don't feel well," but was determined to get out of this state by myself, so I kept up the strokes, making my way to the shallow end, where I could regroup. My heart was slamming.

The enveloping relaxation of floating on my back in a warm pool had gone from delicious to spooky in mere seconds. I remained in the pool, now swimming the width, in order to stay in the shallower water. I was back to the shallow water of the lake at Camp Nageewa. It still felt odd; how come I never noticed before how peculiar this was—this moving atop the water—this effortless effort? Now the groove had been etched and I vigilantly scanned for the feeling and, sure enough, there it was. Make it better, I told myself. Make the negative a positive. Make it interesting. Get a new image. But nothing worked. I was happy for not leaving the pool, and I did stay swimming another forty minutes.

The locker room, usually a chatty place of unashamed nudity and lotions and hairbrushes and soiled towels, was empty. I entered the shower and briefly imagined the concentration camp showers, where gas was pumped in. Damn the mind! Get out! Shake it off!

Once in the car, the sadness hit. Something untainted and uncomplicated had become infected. My experience had been colonized by invading dysfunctional thoughts. My empathy for my patients with OCD and panic grew. Was it a fluke? Just don't return at night, I thought. Swim when other people are there.

Melancholic days passed. I knew it was important to get back on the horse, get back in the pool, and I did. I went for a physical therapy session, but it happened again, even though comforting daylight was streaming through the huge windows and several people were bobbing around and chatting. My physical therapist was standing in the shallow corner, working on her patient notes, half of her body immersed. I confided my experience to her, and we tried various techniques. She was wonderful about it, probably used to various oddities and parasthesias. She even attached a 1½-pound weight to my belt, to help me feel less floaty, which was a little better, but I stayed in the shallow end. We did more snorkel-mask, and the newness of being truly underwater was a distraction from the other feeling.

"Remember," she said kindly, "if you're walking with a cane, at least you're walking."

Ruth is eighty years old and swims on her side as if reaching for a lily pad that is just a bit too far away. Her hearing aid can't accompany her into the pool, so she swims in a quiet whoosh, smiling tolerantly to the chattering others. Her white hair is wrapped in a blue turban. The first time Ruth spoke to me I was flailing about with a flotation belt wrapped around my waist.

"You don't go in the deep end." Her voice dripped with suspicion.

"No, I'm not supposed to," I fibbed. "I mean I'm better down here because of my neck."

She took me in with small dark eyes. Her accent was German. I had often noticed what I assumed to be Slavic planes in her face. She looked like my grandmother and mother. Was she Jewish? Or was she judging me severely from some place of robust Germanic health, of polar dips and bicep curls?

Today Ruth is stepping over and over onto a red plastic tub. Around her ankles are black leather weights. She is wearing her turquoise swimsuit.

I stand in four-foot deep water and move my arms slowly toward the center and then out again, timing my breathing with the motions. Water t'ai chi—the notion is that simulating some normal movements will help my strength and flexibility. Ruth leaves her tub underwater and begins a slow horizontal glide toward me.

"There you are."

Had she been looking for me?

"Does that really do anything?" She shouts.

"Who knows. It's supposed to increase . . ."

"Ah! Can't hear!" She taps her turban, wrapped tightly around her ears to protect her hair, which is bright white and full, in a pageboy cut. She's at the other side of the pool and I close my mouth and nod in her direction.

I notice her feet, shod in mesh slippers, through which I can see her toes, which, unlike the rest of her bent body, are smooth and even. She isn't like the other older folks in the water. She keeps to herself, never joining the aquacise classes, never swapping medical news and talk of grandchildren.

I saw women who looked much like Ruth in an unusual film, *Watermark: The Jewish Swimming Champions Who Defied Hitler*, made in 2004 by Israeli filmmaker Yaron Zilberman, in which he chronicles the Hakoah, a Jewish sports club with a membership of three thousand in Vienna, Austria. It was founded in 1909 as a place for Jewish children to play sports in response to the infamous Aryan Clause, which forbade most Austrian sports clubs from accepting Jewish athletes. In Vienna at that time there were two hundred thousand Jews.

The Hakoah had wrestling and water polo for the boys, who wore a Jewish star on their swim trunks, right by the groin. The male soccer team traveled to the United States, and when they did nine out of eleven stayed in this country because they were offered contracts.

Zilberman finds Hedi, Elisheva, Hanni and Judith (two sisters), and Nanne, who were trained as young girls to swim expertly. They were determined to show how well they could do and did so—the women won many championships. In 1935, they traveled to Tel Aviv for the Maccabia—the Jewish Olympics.

The Berlin Olympics were held in 1936, with the Nazi flag flying and Hitler in power. Judith was to go for swimming. Meanwhile signs in parks read No Dogs & Jews. Although she had trained all her life, Judith refused to go, and her refusal to participate caused her to be banned from ever competing again. At the time, ninety-eight percent of Austrians were Nazis.

In 1938, Germany annexed Austria during the Anschluss and shut down the Hakoah. Mr. Rosenfeld, the devoted president of the swimming club, was on the Gestapo's wanted list—he escaped to London, as did the trainer, and they saved all the swimmers on an illegal ship to Israel. The women scattered all over the world. They stayed in touch throughout the war, through a newsletter, while most everyone they knew perished.

The filmmaker reunited the surviving women, who were in their eighties, and brought them back to Vienna to the pool where they once swam, where they were ultimately banned by the Nazis, but now could swim again. The women, in matching grey bathing suits like the ones they wore when they were young, wiped away tears as they dove into the water. They were the most beautiful mermaids I'd ever seen, buoyant with *heart.*

Even earlier, the first of all Jewish gymnastic clubs was formed in 1895 by German and Austrian Jews living in what was then

Constantinople (now Istanbul) because they were not allowed at the German gymnastic societies, which had "Aryan-only" membership. There was even a phrase: "muscular Judaism." It was first used in the second World Zionist Congress in 1898 when leader Max Nordau, responding to the constant danger of anti-Semitism, called for the creation of "a new Jew." "We Jews possess an exceptional gift for physical activity . . . It is true that our muscles have been weakened and that our attitudes and postures are not always satisfactory . . . but when Jews do engage in sport their defects vanish." Jewish gymnastics clubs were established in Germany, and physical exercise was encouraged for the youth.

Diminishing pools of water leading toward the light. Grey heads bobbing, brains suspended in tanks.

Fantasy sweeps over the surface of the water.

On my back, I am the wealthy philanthropist: the infirm and aged glide nearby—my generous gift—they come in to use my facilities. Skin folds wink at me, thighs brush forlornly, swish swish into the depths, to commence the glacial stroll.

A temporary ceasefire on gravity's war—all muscles equal here; to move too fast is rude.

My rifle, snug in its canvas case, leans against the wall in my closet. Holding my neck in the various and necessary required positions for shooting became just too painful. If I ever took it up again, I'd definitely need some refresher lessons. There's every likelihood that I will, because since I've been boxing, my neck doesn't hurt anymore.

18

still a man's world

"Hey," John says on my answering machine, "I don't like the sound of this—this prosthetics business. That doesn't sound good."

No, John, not prosthetics—*orthotics.*

I've now spent a small fortune on custom-made orthotics because while my neck may not hurt anymore, my right calf aches like nothing I've ever felt, with a sudden throbbing so intense it takes my breath away. The whole leg feels heavy, there's some tingling on the bottom of my foot, and no amount of stretching or massage helps. Tylenol, Advil, Aspirin—nothing touches the pain, and it's so intermittent what would be the point.

After the day John noticed my boxing stance was weak and he instructed me to keep my right leg extended further back, the pain got worse. I had upped my lessons to twice a week, and then I had to stop completely because of the pain. I searched boxing sites on the Internet for tales of boxer's woes. While runners and tennis players discussed common injuries in forums everywhere, all I could find for boxers were descriptions of head injuries and pugilistic dementia.

"I'm not getting an artificial limb!" I reassure John.

"I don't hear from you enough. You gotta call me, baby—otherwise I'm gonna worry."

"Well, I can't box, so . . ."

"Hey! We don't have to just get together and pound on each other."

"You're right. I'm sorry. But will you take me back when I'm ready?"

"Are you kidding me? I love you. You're hurt. You're on the bench. You'll be back. Every fighter's got some crazy string of injuries and, more often than not, it all works out. Your pal Sam Dane? She's got two bum shoulders, a bad knee, a groin pull."

It took a while to get to the orthotics. First my internist, who screwed up her little healthy face into a grimace of distaste and disapproval when I mentioned boxing, ordered an ultrasound to rule out a clot. A friendly technician from Iceland administered the test while we discussed Bjork and other Icelandic rock 'n roll artists. I was nervous and appeared so interested in Iceland she gave me her family's address for when I visited. *As if.*

On to Keith, a physical therapist who didn't grimace and who's done some boxing and is curious about doing some training with John. "There's gotta be a ring, though," he says, indicating that he's a serious contender. I go home with back exercises for what he thinks might be sciatica, but that yields no improvement whatsoever.

Trim and enthusiastic Lisa is a personal trainer and a devotee of the Aaron Mates method of two-minute stretches. "What? You're not warming up before you box?" It does suddenly seem ridiculous. John's never been big on the medical end of things; he often says he's there to give me a session of intense boxing and that's it. I think he expected me to warm up before we started, but I was often fitting the lessons into a tightly packed day of patients. Lisa starts me on a strengthening routine to build up my legs and my overall cardiovascular capacity. "Powerwalk!" she commands, and soon Griffin and Sabine's little tongues are hanging out farther as they try to keep up with me in the woods.

I'm a cooperative client, but soon I'm halting short walks through the supermarket to surreptitiously raise my aching leg onto a shelf. I miss John. I miss boxing. I miss being able to stroll happily to the frozen food section.

Kristin and I talk about our infirmities over coffee at Starbucks. She's got a bad knee, but she's trying alternative methods before giving in to the recommended surgery. She also broke her leg twice and it never healed properly. I love having someone to commiserate with, but we may as well be in rocking chairs on the porch of a rest home or walking slowly through the aquatherapy pool discussing our grandchildren.

I receive a letter from my disapproving internist who is retiring to Cape Cod. She's probably got some grandchildren there. I switch to Dr. Lane, who sees me right away as a professional courtesy. My latest theory, buoyed up by more Internet research, is that I have intermittent claudication, which is a peripheral arterial disease, like hardening of the arteries in the legs, or chronic exertional compartment syndrome (a trendier version of shin splints), in which muscles swell and there's no room for fascia and veins and arteries. The calf is a very compact unit, like the forearm.

Dr. Lane studied geriatric medicine in her residency and she doesn't think I fit the profile for claudication—I don't smoke or have coronary problems, and my leg pulses are healthy and "bounding." She doesn't grimace when I mention boxing, but she does ask if it involves blows to the head. She sends me to Dr. Ronan, an orthopedist.

I'm really in the medical maze now and it is dizzying.

Dr. Ronan is the first one to look down at my feet and notices significant pronation, which could be twisting tendons and muscles.

"Could any of this have gotten worse because of the broken ankle and foot from a few years ago?" I ask. *I felt like a great endless scream through nature.*

"It's possible. I'm referring you to a pedorthist for orthotics. That should help."

So bones heal, but . . .

Orthotics—the very word summons up images of legs with swollen ankles taking small, laboriously slow steps, dressed in ugly functional shoes with Velcro bands. My grandmother took an eternity to move one leg, in a beige, rolled, thick support-stocking, up into the car. We impatient kids rolled our eyes. But now that my own membership in AARP is becoming more bona fide than ever, I feel a surge of sympathy for her. We are not so different, she and I. We probably never were.

My months of boxing are starting to seem like a careless journey in a dream. I am losing the girl who could roundhouse kick and shriek in delight, the healthy doppelganger. The aches-and-pains body is taking over, as if a pod has been placed by my gymbag. *Invasion of the Body Snatchers.*

Every day I add an hour of training time to the orthotics, which are like medieval torture devices. Tiny elves are hammering away at all the bones in my legs with small deliberate movements. According to Ken the pedorthist, who outfits the New Haven hockey team, I may have exacerbated my problem by boxing in the wrong shoes, and doing it on hard surfaces. *Like when I swam around the edges of the above-ground pool, craning and straining my neck.*

I just want to box again and be able to walk fast.

"This is all good, actually," Ken the pedorthist says, slipping my check for over $800 for three different pairs into his tweed sports jacket. "If you hadn't started boxing, you'd just get older and start to have pain in your feet and legs and think, oh well, that's aging, and just adapt to it, when you don't have to.

"And by the way," he adds, "it's genetic."

"Great," I say.

So what do I do while I'm on the bench? I watch other people fight. I go to the gym on a Sunday when several burly men are setting up the new ring, which was donated by a police athletic league (now Keith the physical therapist can come and box), and I try to be unobtrusive but helpful, offering to run to Home Depot for last-minute supplies. I take Ryan, the fifteen-year-old fighter whose dad is banging ring posts, to Subway for food for the gang. All these young guys are remarkably polite.

"So you box, too?" Ryan asks, with respect, as I'm negotiating the busy Post Road. I've never driven a fifteen-year-old boy anywhere before. Back at the gym, John dives into a funk because he's frustrated that it's all taking so long and, dismayed by the huge size of the ring, becomes impatient. How can I soothe him? I try some physical things—arm around the shoulder, quick neck rub. He's glum. I try to take my cues from John's son Hunter, who is keeping his distance; he's probably been through this a million times. It's the first time I've seen this so clearly in John. *Hi, Daddy. Please don't be upset. Don't upset your father.*

I go to the gym one evening after work, summoned by John because the *Connecticut Post* is sending reporters and photographers to see the boxing group John runs, called "Aging Bulls," in action. I don't even take my gloves so that I won't be tempted into the ring because I'm still in a lot of pain. So I bring my laptop and, while others are getting wrapped, I set up a few chairs outside the ring and plug in.

There's Jenni, Sue, Joan—all impressively fierce in the ring, and John calls out commands. They fight in pairs, hitting each other's gloves. Sue, the women's studies teacher, who like a lot of us struggles with body image, may not have the goal of sparring, but she is a dynamic puncher, moving fast and hitting hard. So is her fighting partner, another plus-sized woman who's got an attractive outfit on—low-cut tank top, white shorts. Her arms are solid and tanned. I get my interview done with the reporter, explaining that I'm on the bench for a while. I am peering through the venetian blinds at the popular girls playing softball.

Jenni pops out of the ring.

"Can I get you a cup of tea?"

That's it—I'm like the visiting auntie.

I pack up my laptop and skulk out without saying goodbye.

Then next Sunday it's "Open Boxing" at the club for eight fighters who are preparing for their fights. I sit on a folding chair and watch men fight, up close and personal. Ryan and Manuel are competing next month and they are looking good. Ryan's T-shirt is drenched. I watch their legs, their feet, their shoes, wondering why they are not disabled like me. *Oh that's right. They're young.* John strides back and forth, calling out instructions and observations. He never misses a thing. After the round ends, there's conditioning with a heavyball. The idea is to throw it against your partner's stomach and vice versa to harden yourself up and get ready to take punches, a purposeful *bombardmen*t. I'm practically salivating with the desire to be in the ring punching.

And then it hits me, as if for the first time, from the vantage point of "outside" the ring, that aside from the Aging Bulls class, this sport is so much a man's world. I'd never seen it so vividly before. When I was in the fever pitch of private boxing lessons, the larger world didn't exist—the real men, their muscles, their attitudes, their club. Now they're before me in their glory, teasing each other, sweating, joking, hitting. It is not my world.

Hey lady, get out of the way, I can't see my son fighting.

A discussion begins about a name for the team. John asks me what I think of "Trauma Center" for a name. I don't like it. Big burly wrestler guy whose feminine wife is watching from the sidelines, too, looks at me, looks at John, and says "That's right, you should get a woman's point of view."

I shoot him a withering look.

Woman's point of view?

I've gotten professional boxing lessons from a former fighter and now I'm offering a "woman's point of view"? The men start talking about ultimate cage-fighting, the latest trend.

"I'd love to get a cage," John says.

"You just got a ring—you finally got the ring, and now you want a cage?" I call out, like a ridiculously chastising mother of an ungrateful teenager. *Bubbie Goes Boxing.*

Two huge guys drop to the floor, and I watch the triangular squeezes and passionate embraces. I could be witnessing a demonstration of the Kama Sutra. It's like Oliver Reed and Alan Bates in *Women in Love*, and their nude wrestling scene in front of the crackling fire, so shocking back in 1969 in Ken Russell's film adaptation of Lawrence's novel. In cage-fighting, fighters try to topple each other and get strongholds so fierce and tight the loser taps his opponent's chest to signal, "Uncle, I've had enough—stop!" That's how it works in Brazilian jujitsu, where you grapple your opponent into submission. John puts on a huge black leather shield that straps around the back, so that he can be kicked by Mike, the twenty-three-year-old salesman who is going to make his debut as a mixed martial arts fighter. John's coaching him for the fight. Mike is an adorable guy, with dark curly hair and tattoos, and he's strutting around yelling gruesome details about what he'd like to do to his opponent.

"If you kick him in the knees and he goes down like that," John shouts, "I'll shriek like a fourteen-year-old girl!"

Whomp! John barely escapes being tripped by Mike's big leg.

"And I can't wait until the fight's over, so all the testosterone-inspired dirty jokes can stop!" John says.

I'm peeking through yet another set of venetian blinds, this time at men in a raw and sensuous element, eager to make intense contact with each other. They would be appalled, but the word homoerotic dances through my mind. How could it not? It's like I'm in the locker room and men are stripping down and snapping each other's butts with wet towels. I'm the wandering female reporter, averting my eyes shyly as I make my way through the sweaty hard bodies. Still I leap at the chance to throw a heavy medicine ball against Mike's abs while his bemused girlfriend, cute, young, and trim, looks on. I must look like a demented grandmother.

Pickles, anyone?

John was particularly pumped at the "Open Boxing" because earlier that week he was asked to come down on a few hours notice to Madison Square Garden. They were filming *The Main Event*, a wrestling show on NBC and John was asked to pretend to train a wrestler and get him ready for a boxing match—and the match was with Evander Holyfield.

I taped the show and watched it the next day. John and another trainer, his longtime friend Harry, emerge out of smoke and darkness, music blaring, flanking their wrestler, carrying buckets, wearing shiny short robes. Wrestling is America's crazy fix—full of characters, outfits, pounding, scandals, bravado. It's a show, even more so than boxing, and John and Harry shout encouragement at their wrestler and then welcome him back to the corner. Again, it's men, men, men, and since this is wrestling, and this is pro, voluptuous bikini-clad woman strut around the ring holding up signs between rounds. This is the only role for women here, botoxed, boob implanted, shaved, and wearing skimpy bikini bottoms and high heels.

I don't want access to this club, but I'm curious about how men get to have these celebrated worlds of public and physical contact while women can merely sit around a table at *The View* and kibbitz. Of course there are Venus and Serena, the Connecticut Huskies, many fabulous women athletes. But this is different. This is my chosen game, and I had forgotten something very essential about it or maybe I never really knew. In my private lessons, and at the very amateur level, I had been in a bubble. And of course I'm bitter and restless because I'm not boxing.

Are there any female Johns?

The *Sunday New Haven Register* says yes. The U.S. Postal Service has become my guide, a shaman to rival Carlos Castaneda's Don Juan. All I have to do is walk to my mailbox and the next road of my journey will be revealed. There in the paper I see a full-page article about a fifty-year-old domestic violence survivor who is coaching men and women up in Stafford Springs, Connecticut. Her name is Terry Tumminia-Edwards, and they say she's a firecracker, a dynamo who holds down three jobs, a tireless champion of boxing. It's time, more than time, for me to see a woman like her in action. It's a little hard to track her down, as it was with John. But she herself answers her phone and says yes without any hesitation. Yes, I can come and watch her train her boxers and interview her for my new radio feature on boxing. John has already appeared on the show, and we talked for forty-five minutes about bare-knuckle boxing, Muay Thai, aggression, and discipline. We got some very favorable responses.

Terry is thrilled and eager for the publicity.

It's the perfect thing to do while I'm on the bench.

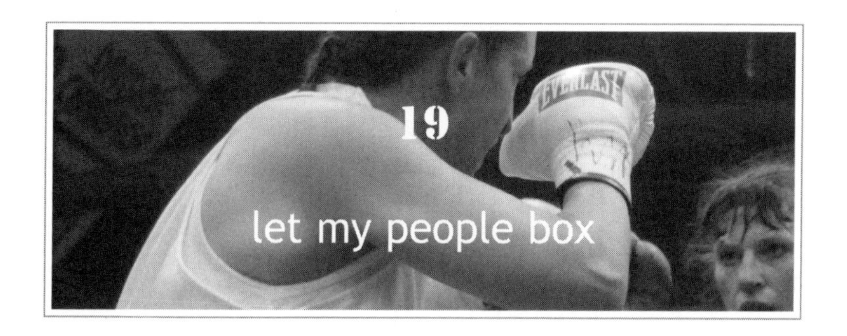

19

let my people box

"We want to rule out any zebras," my orthopedist was saying, when he suggested an MRI.

"Zebras?" I asked, as if this was an actual medical finding.

He laughed. "Oh, just, you know . . . anything rare and unexpected."

He did battle with the insurance company to authorize the MRI, which turned out to be normal; this left me reassured, but still in pain. I reinvested my energy into Internet research. And one day, while experimentally wearing a compression stocking on my right calf, the pain temporarily receded. I found a vascular specialist who did a more elaborate series of tests and, in a doppler ultrasound, found the cause of my problem. I had "reflux," which sounded distinctly unsexy, like I was going to need Tums. Venus insuffiency, to be specific. A lack of romance? A damaged valve somewhere in the anterior tibial vein valve, possibly aggravated by the break in my ankle. When I stood or walked for long periods, blood that flowed to the calves via the arteries from the heart, was having trouble getting back up through the veins, so there was a pooling effect. This is what made my leg feel like it was going to explode, and this is why the only relief came from putting my leg up.

"I guess you stumbled onto your treatment," the doctor said, and ordered more compression stockings, prescription strength. In the homecare section of my pharmacy, I was initiated into the ritual by a dark-haired, fast-talking "specialist" who told me I should never, ever, ever stop wearing them. She rolled her eyes when I said I was hoping that exercise would help. We were sitting in a storage room because some other unfortunate venus-insufficiency sufferer was being fitted in the designated instruction room.

"Here, let's get you some gloves—hmmm, you have small hands, okay, take these rubber gloves, see, you'll be buying a pair, and they have ridges, see, and then gather, roll, pull, stretch, and smooth out over your calf." She waited.

I snapped on the gloves like a surgeon and folded the stockings over until she said "there!" and then I began the slow unfurling upward over my calf, remembering my first lesson with John, a very different pair of gloves, and my eyeballs sweating, my heart pounding, and my confident strutting in the park. *So that's an hour of boxing.*

"Wear them every day, don't stop," she cautioned.

"What do people do in the summer?" I asked.

"Just deal with the pain, I guess."

Mine was not an uncommon problem, but it had taken eight months to figure out. The doctor said I could still box, but he couldn't guarantee that it wouldn't cause pain, and, in fact, as months went on, I found that there was no real cure for the pain. It was reduced by the stockings, but my real hope lay in strengthening the bejeesus out of that calf muscle because it might help the arteries and veins do their work better. No doctor suggested this, but that's my plan.

Here I am, Grandma. I've got the support stockings now, too. How cruel I had been, impatient as you walked slowly and hoisted your leg into the car, judging you from my remote and illusory throne of sturdiness. I descend now into the warm waters for the glacial stroll with you and the others at the pool. The Hakoah women are there, too, eager to teach me how to really swim.

"I'm off to the reading room," John says, grabbing a *Ring* magazine and heading into the bathroom. I take a healthy swig of water, crush the bottle, and throw it in the garbage. I'm thinking about whether I should go to the mall and continue my search for the T-shirt that will make me look smaller, the workout pants that will elongate my legs. I guess I don't hear the door of the gym open and don't realize I am slipping into another fantasy.

"Well! This is vexing. A female combatant?!"

I turn toward the voice—can't imagine how he appeared so quickly, but swiftness was one of Daniel Mendoza's greatest attributes. He's bare-chested, with serious biceps, and he's wearing very worn but clean pants that taper just below the knee. They're made of some flannel or cotton, very thick, and there are two buttons at the waist. Across his crotch is a triangle with a button on either side. It's like an inverted diaper. Tall socks meet the bottom of the pants, or knickers—what to call them? And pointy leather shoes with bows adorn his feet.

"Can I be of aid?" he continues. "Are you being threatened by that rogue?"

"No, thanks. He's actually my coach," I say, taking a moment to look at his, well, enormous nose. He's quite swarthy, too, and his sideburns are so far into his cheeks it's like they're reaching for that nose. All of his thick burly hair is combed forward from a point at the back of his head. His lips are full, and there's a bit of sadness in his eyes.

"Well then, I have many questions. I think I have a right to call myself the father of the science of boxing. Prizefighting had lain dormant for years, until myself and Mr. Humphries revived it through our three contests for supremacy. The science of pugilism has been patronized ever since. You've heard the poem: 'Is this the Jew of whom my fancy cherished so beautiful a waking dream?' That was me!"

I played along and nodded.

"Tis I! And while I am in your presence, we'd best make good use. I'm off to Ireland to lecture on the pugilistic science. I don't condone your femininity in this pursuit, but I can offer my considerable expertise."

Boxing tips from Daniel Mendoza! I rewrap my hands as fast as I can.

"But do tell me, miss, what are those leather balloons?"

"Oh my god, that's right—you all didn't have boxing gloves until 1860. You just did it with your fists!" I say.

"Bare-knuckle, most certainly." Mendoza assumes the pose I'd only seen in silent movies and antique photographs and sketches—arms and fists outstretched as if a horse has risen on its hinds legs and is ready to prance forward. He makes tight little circles with his fists.

"So what did they call you?" I ask.

"The Star of Israel, sometimes the Light of the East—this was after my first battle with Mr. Humphries. I was paid five guineas, having won of course, and then they gave me the appellation. Miss, do not think me impertinent, but could you be Jewish as well?"

"Yes."

"Ah, now I understand. You have no man and you are threatened by the slurs—we are both in the battle against injustice and prejudice." Mendoza picks up one of the boxing gloves and throws it into the air, as if to feel its weight.

"Well, I don't think I have actually experienced the same . . . ," I pick up the other glove, wondering whether he might actually put them on.

"I would never let my wife fight; in fact I promised her I would quit it, but there were times, Miss, so hard to resist . . . I was apprenticed to a tea-maker, and a porter came to the house with a delivery. I offered him a tip, and the porter demanded more, then he made some anti-Semitic remarks about the family I worked for. So I took him out into the street. A ring being consequently formed in the street, we immediately set to, and after a severe contest of about three-quarters of an hour my opponent yielded. My second was the esteemed Mr. Richard Humphries. More of him later. Well, the neighborhood was ablaze with the news of this battle and next thing I knew I was matched to another man, and of course I won. But my employer wasn't too pleased by Mendoza's activities, and fired him. So I was relieved of my duties quite often, Miss. It was hard to make a proper living. But that's over now! I can obtain fifty pounds for each theater appearance in my demonstrations."

"We shan't use the leather balloons for now, Miss. Come step to me here, and let's take a look, shall we?"

I stand next to him. Boxing's first Jewish superstar is not super-tall. He's around five foot seven, and probably weighs 160 pounds. We're both middleweights; that's another thing we've got in common. I think of Hank Greenberg's story of towering over most Jewish men, who were five three, five four as he entered, all six foot seven of him, the synagogue on Yom Kippur to pray instead of playing professional baseball. The worshippers stood, uncharacteristically, and applauded this giant for just walking through the door.

"Miss, a boxer needs to be in a state of equilibrium so that you can move to the left or the right with ease, placing yourself in a diagonal line, so as to position the pit of the stomach out of your adversary's reach. Both knees must be bent, the left leg advanced, and the arms directly before your throat or chin. I see that you are short-armed, so your superiority over your antagonist will consist in close fighting; you must therefore endeavor to get within the compass of his arms, and aim short, straight blows that will reach him before he can strike at you and, if he does strike, his fists will go over your shoulder."

"Dan," I say, "this is just what John is teaching me. I'll never be a real puncher because I'm not tall. I can't do long powerful hits, but I can try to get in close, stay close, and keep boxing, inside."

"Well, if your adversary is ignorant of boxing—that's what we'll be hoping for. Then he—or she, I suppose—will be awkward and slovenly, and you can take your advantage. In 1780, I dispatched Harry the Coalheaver in forty rounds."

I start throwing punches at my image in the mirror, shadow-boxing with all my might. "Forty rounds—Dan, we don't go that long these days."

"What are you inferring? Cowardice?"

"No! No, I mean we have rules. A three-minute round, for example."

"Ah, cowardice, as I thought. We fought until one man lay down, and that took as long as it took. A real battle. Now look sharp now. Parry this riposte by catching my wrist with your right fists, and strike a backhanded blow across my face with your left hand."

A flurry of giant hands come at me and I slip, weave, and then just frankly step out of the way, to my left.

"I invented that!" Mendoza shouts. "That defensive maneuver. The way you stepped to the left. I didn't fancy the hard punching; I was the expert at many fast punches and defensive movements, and they served me well. I used this in my second battles with Mr. Humphries."

"This Mr. Humphries," I pant, while trying again to parry his riposte, whatever that was, "you seem kind of obsessed with him."

"Well I don't think he truly won that first battle, for I was ill and rather melancholy about my loss of my son."

"Oh, I'm so sorry."

". . . and yet he insisted I fight. I endeavored to establish another match, and we just could not set the terms. First it was this, then that."

I see that I have to get Mendoza off this subject, so I switch gears.

"Is it true that you were a bounty hunter for a while?"

"Yes, Miss, but that was a tawdry profession. I left it after a time, although I was excellent at this field. Wouldn't you rather hear about my fighting for the King of England?"

The toilet flushed from the other end of the gym. John would be coming back.

"Of course, but what I really want to know is why don't more people know that the Father of Pugilism was Jewish?"

"Ah," said Daniel Mendoza, pushing his dark curls off his face and sitting down on the weight bench. "You know, my dear lady, we were not supposed to be tough. We were the scholars. Of course, some men of turbulent and vindictive dispositions have made a bad use of their pugilistic power, and, as Shakespeare says, 'It is good to have a giant's strength, but merciless to use it like a giant.' But for self-defense, which goes back to the Roman gladiators, I have created the scientific study, I suppose, for people like you. Although you're not, pardon, what I imagined. But we cannot stand by while the slurs fly. I could not tolerate it. I do not fathom how anyone could. We are as good and strong as anyone you might bring forward. Just let me have an hour with a man and I will educate him on his own protection. I am the Greatest Fighter!"

"*I am the greatest*," said Muhammad Ali.

We stand looking at each other, our dark eyes locked, peering into each other like animals on opposite sides of cages in a zoo.

"Look after yourself on the cobbles, my dear," Mendoza says.

"Hey, baby, my pugilistic progeny, my diva of destruction, why are your wraps still on?" John calls out as he approaches me.

"I was just, I mean . . . I wanted another round. Did you know that in the old days they just went till they dropped?" I asked.

Mendoza was gone.

"Sure. And the original ring was just a circle in the sand. Men fought with their bare-knuckles. But you're not going another round, baby. You're done for the day."

20

poet laureate of plainview

I'm no stranger to unpredictable story lines. Every day people infiltrate my psyche with their rambling narratives, and though they are not tales of scaling Mount Everest or chewing off an arm to get out of a bear trap or escaping a prison camp in the dead of night, they are as important and dramatic to my patients as any sound-bite proclamation on network news. In particular, our culture's fascination with midlife transformations keeps disproving F. Scott Fitzgerald's claim that "there are no second acts in American lives." Joseph Campbell's idea of the hero's quest never falls out of vogue. We may not be faced with dangerous treks through murky caves, armed with small lanterns as we search for helpful animal guides, but once our AARP bulletin arrives in the mail, we can use all the help we can get.

Everyone is the heroic protagonist of their own life.

I turned over my boxing stone when I persuaded a former middleweight champ in New Haven, Connecticut, to "take me on." This is the way things happen for most of us who are not living loud, highly publicized, or dramatic lives, when we find our joy, our souls, our passions—it's through quiet stories of challenge, obstacles, persistence, and unexpected or accidental convergences.

Weird stones rub out assumptions and preconceived notions, especially when we finally see the imprint of their true shape in the dirt underneath. I make no apology for the fact that boxing can be violent and certainly aggressive; that's part of its allure and excitement. It is also true that boxing, especially in the amateur class, is not *as* violent as professional boxing (we get to wear head-gear and fight fewer rounds), and can teach kids and adults a huge array of life skills. It promotes community, can keep kids off the streets by teaching them discipline, helping them endure setbacks and frustration and develop goals. Boxing has long fascinated writers and historians with its themes of race, class, corruption, good versus evil, the role of primal instincts and aggression in our lives, the plight of the underdog, and the qualities of courage and "heart."

A boxer needs some rage. My father probably would have made a good boxer. He could have channeled his fury and, in so doing, "left it in the ring." Boxing would have taught my dad how to keep his cool, develop composure (if you get flustered when someone is coming at you, the odds are you're going to take a hit), and make his anger work for him rather than against him.

I knew at least some of why my father was angry. He never got to do what he really wanted, and he had a severe case of what Alain de Botton calls "status anxiety."

I knew some of why the early Jewish boxers were angry. They were picked on constantly and everyone assumed they were weaklings. Benny Leonard, lightweight champion from 1917 to 1925, was constantly in a turf war with the Irish in the poor neighborhoods of Chicago. Barney Ross suffered a horrible trauma when he was thirteen—he witnessed a botched holdup when robbers shot and killed his father. His mother had a nervous breakdown and, when the family split apart, Barney's younger sib-lings were sent off to an orphanage. And then there were the sordid, sad tales of Jews forced to box to win the right to live one more day. During the German occupation of Poland in 1939, fighter Harry Haft was captured by the Nazis. In the camp he was forced to bare-knuckle fight for the pleasure of the guards, and losers were often immediately executed. Harry never lost a fight and the sadistic guards called him "The Jew Animal." He escaped the camp, and in America became a professional boxer. Salamo Arouch, who died in 2009 at the age of 86, was a Greek-born Jewish boxer who survived the Auschwitz death camp by winning fight after fight against fellow prisoners, as Nazi guards placed bets. His story was the basis for the 1989 movie, *Triumph of the Spirit*.

I knew why my coach John was angry. His manipulative alcoholic mother was a rager who controlled him and his brother throughout their childhood. Why was I angry? Was it because we were all helpless before our father's rage? Because my mother's voice, when she did speak, seemed barely a whisper? Unlike my parents, and so many of the immigrants of their generation, I'd been able to get an education and develop a career that I liked. Sure, I'd had my hurts and disappointments, but I'd had so much more freedom than either of my parents.

Or maybe anger isn't the issue—maybe it's competition. If you win, someone else has to lose. After all, sports wouldn't exist without winners and losers. You have to be willing to go beyond someone else to participate in sports. In my family, if you had drive and hurt someone else along the way, even not deliberately, you were deemed selfish and horrible. Assimilation required suppression of the self. Don't say too much good about yourself or god will punish you. Don't stand out. Don't call attention to yourself. Don't email the gods.

As a little girl, my fights were about getting out of challenges that I *made* into fights—being truant on gym days to avoid the sadistic gym teacher, pretending to have my period to avoid swimming lessons at summer camp. I would get close to the edges of life's excitement and potential successes and decide there was too much to fear. Well-meaning, comforting hands were always there to pull me back down into the well. *It's okay, it's okay, come back home. We're frightened, too.*

As an adult, I had days when a walk to the mailbox without panic was a triumph, when driving across a bridge made me positively exultant. Those were rough times. As I write this, I hear the whisper of the censoring gremlin on my shoulder. *What are your patients going to think? Your colleagues?* All of us who jettison a narrative, or some portion thereof, out into the universe have spent time with that creature, if we're telling the truth. Sometimes it's in the form of a haughty parent, one eyebrow arched in disapproval, or a seemingly blemishless authority who stares blankly at your tormented words, as if to say, "*Uh, I don't understand . . . why didn't you just . . . get over it?*" To make matters worse, there is the pack of wild dog gurus (Deepak Chopra, Tom Cruise!) who assure us that everything can be overcome, once we are "open" to change.

If you've spent any time at all in the seductive arms of panic, you know that it is not just your body that enacts its "fight or flight" repetition. Your head gets in the way—with its crystalline imagination and capacity for self-torture and imagined dangers. As a result, I'm often been too cerebral, cognitively flooded, introspective, dreamy, ambivalent, paralyzed by nuances. When John teaches me now to slip, weave, block, and feint, what am I literally doing? I'm getting my head out of the way! I'm leaving obsessions behind and entering a state of flow: all things immediate and with consequences. In my work as a psychotherapist, I dwell in a land of ambiguity where people beat themselves up. I try to help them fight off the blows inside their heads that they inflict upon themselves. Sometimes I'm the fight manager, and sometimes I am the stand-in opponent, learning their particular fight so I can help them. What are you angry about? I ask. Who are you angry at? What do you really want?

When John took me on, he said it was because he saw something in my eyes—a persistence, a determination—that I just would not give up. He may as well have lifted me up into the air and jettisoned my being into a new and heavenly realm. *I was not a quitter. I never really was.*

If you look closely, you can see that everyone is fighting all the time, with loved ones, with themselves, with traffic, with opponents both real and imagined. Parents grab their children's arms harshly, people argue with each other on the street, corporate executives lobby for power, politicians push their ideas forward, and countries go to war.

I don't know if I'll be able to meet my goal of sparring with another woman my size, but I'm not going to give up. I bought an exercise bike, and I'm trying to do at least forty minutes a day because Sam Dane agrees with me that if I work the heck out of that calf muscle, I can help the blood flow and have less pain. I'm taking pine-bark extract because I researched some encouraging studies on venus insufficiency.

I hope, as John promises, that "we'll always be boxing."

One day John called me up to suggest that I work the corner with him, and that's how I came to be a part of Manuel's victory. I never could have imagined I would ever be holding a bucket under a young fighter's face, and cheering him on, but I'm sure I'll be doing it again. I've covered professional fights and sat with other media types pounding away on their laptops. With my media pass I can get up close to the ring and take pictures. John and I have started a feature on my radio show, "In Your Corner." We interview boxers and authors and sportswriters. We've had Jack Cavanaugh, David Margolick, Yuri Foreman, Bert Randolph Sugar, Angelo Dundee, and Lucia Rijker.

Boxing has made me smarter. I know more about history, I'm more aware of everything around me, I'm more confident, and I make fewer assumptions about things and people I don't understand.

I can hear Yiddish now without cringing. It's an amazing language, full of life and humor. I still think about Barney Ross's first wife, Pearl Siegel, and my mother, Regina Siegel. I want to do more intensive genealogy.

Recently, my sister Mikki brought me a surprising gift for my birthday—a beautiful, exquisitely detailed miniature, a scroll with tiny writing on it, in a thin glass tube. A *mezuzah*. The frame is a rustic metal, which will go nicely with the warm Tuscan colors of my kitchen. It's a welcome contrast to the mysterious, painted-over mounds that marked our childhood apartments.

I've been told Rabbi Tellman is a progressive, hip rabbi. When I call him, he even picks up his own phone. "I'm writing a book," I say, "It's about boxing, it's about Judaism; it's stirred up a lot of feelings . . . about the past . . . my family. I have questions. I think I need . . . to talk to a rabbi," I stammer.

"Boxing to Judaism? Hmm." He pauses. "Well, I do like to talk," he says. "How's next Wednesday?"

When Wednesday came, I wondered what it would be like to walk into a synagogue for the first time in so many years. I half expected to hear the poignant wail of a cantor and be swept up into a crowd of welcoming familiar faces. Instead, the synagogue was quite empty. It looked like a rundown elementary school, and I got lost wandering its halls looking for the rabbi's office.

Finally, a woman emerged from a glass-enclosed cubicle and pointed toward the offices. Rabbi Tellman emerged, looked at me blankly, then gestured toward a book-lined room with threadbare carpeting. As my tale spilled out, I was aware of his distraction, which made me all the more disorganized. *I'm a Jew. I've come home! Where's the welcome wagon stocked with bagels and lox?* He mentioned a few books I might read. He offered some history. I now pictured his congregation, an intact family, relationships honed over decades, skeptical of newcomers. *You're not a real Jew . . . you mean you don't fast on Yom Kippur?*

"A question, Rabbi Tellman, is it true every orthodox man says a prayer every day thanking god he was not born a woman? Is it considered so horrid to be a woman?"

"This one I can answer," Rabbi Tellman says. "The prayer relates to the fact that women are not obligated to say as many commandments as men because they are deemed to be in the home, and caretakers of the children, which is a time-bound commitment. Some of the commandments are time-bound, and so the women cannot do them. The men are allowed to fulfill more commandments, which is a joy and a pleasure, so they are grateful."

A dollop of clarity. Now would come the invitation to attend a service, to study great books with him, like when John first said there would be a second boxing lesson. Instead Rabbi Tellman stood and moved toward his coat, draped over a nearby chair.

"I'm sorry, I must go to a funeral."

"Oh, I hope it wasn't someone very close," I offered, as he buttoned his long black coat.

"Unfortunately, it was."

"I thought you seemed . . . tired." *Oh god! Who am I to observe the rabbi.* But our discussion had been so strained and he looked so uncomfortable, I went for the gentle jab of reality.

"Well," he said without much feeling, "it's the life of a rabbi."

I'd gone to the synagogue because picking up your weird stone is a commitment. You want to see it through, wherever it leads you. I was still working my way back into the ring to box, and hoped that in the meantime I'd have the promise of something neat and tidy like *Wednesdays with Rabbi Tellman* (my own *Tuesdays with Morrie*)—in other words, not end at all, but begin again.

What did I know?

No, things didn't happen quite that way.

I haven't hung the mezuzah. It requires two exceptionally tiny nails that I need to find at a hardware store.

I haven't become an observant Jew, and I haven't read more about Judaism. What I am reading is *But He Was Good to His Mother: The Lives and Crimes of Jewish Gangsters*. But, as they say, a funny thing happened. My eldest sister called one day, breathless with a discovery.

"I found something," she said, barely able to contain her excitement. "A batch of poems. You're not gonna believe this."

"Oh? By whom?" In a recurrent and fruitless quest for longed-for domestic order, each of us sisters occasionally forages through old boxes, chests, and filing cabinets, hoping to purge the moldy and unnecessary. Helpful magazine articles call it "de-cluttering," a cure for what appears to have become an epidemic of disorganization, given the proliferation of advice. Occasionally we'd find writings we'd done in earlier years.

"Daddy."

"Whaaa?"

"He was putting them together in his eighties, for a collection to give to us. It says, 'Dedicated to my three fillies.' There's maybe fifteen of them. God, he was a funny writer, very clever. It makes me sad to think I didn't give him enough credit while he was alive."

"Please, send them to me. I'd love to see them."

I awaited the arrival of the package. I could have returned to Rabbi Tellman, fully cognizant that I'd met him on a bad day, and that of course there were many ways to study Judaism or make new connections.

Sometimes it takes a while to realize that you no longer need a coach.

When the express package arrived, I ripped open the mailer and did a quick once-over of some of the titles: *Saratoga 1946* (about his love of the track), *Three for the Money* (about his three daughters), *Blind Date* (about meeting his last wife), *I Love New Yorkers*, *Little Miss Spider* (about his girlfriend who worked for Murder, Inc.), *The Life of a Salesman*, *All Kidding Aside* (about World War II), *Avoiding Alzheimer's*, *Hurrah and Goodbye* (about aging). These long, rhyming odes were not the best poetry in the world, but his distinctive voice was there, and the wit and insight. And then there it was—one final poem at the bottom of the stack.

About a boxing match.

The Legend of Blue Eyes and Big Nose

by Jay Klein, the Poet Laureate of Plainview

There is an old adage that says, "He who
fights and runs away, will live to fight another day."
His credo was "fight, but stay, come what may, or you'll
be running away from life, forever and a day."

Those were the days, when your claim to fame
was a passport to Brooklyn, and a given nickname.
There was "chowderhead" and "bullfrog" to mention a few
and ones that were whispered out of hearing and view
some carried it to glory, others to shame,
but, as the bard once asked, "What's in a name?"

Jay was born with blue eyes and a large proboscis
Family facsimile of his grandfather Moses.
His friends called him "blue eyes" and there were those
who behind his back, dubbed him "big nose."
He felt his nose was Romanesque when seen by light
and even much smaller when seen by night.

"You have a nose full of quarters," smirked "scrambled eggs"
So labeled because of his knobby knees and weird scrawny legs.
Jay decked him quickly, and after he won
it always reminded him of his favorite pun;
he had unscrambled scrambled eggs
and left him well done.

The last period bell had rung in the high school gym
Jay started to leave but, coming toward him,
a menacing figure was blocking his path.
It was the head gym teacher, face wreathed in wrath
he was Bartholomew Bass, the heavyweight champ of his college class,
popularly known to all as "Mr. Bad Ass."

Bass blew his whistle. "No one is to go.
All will remain and witness a boxing show.
To fight in my class is an unpardonable sin
observe this and you will think twice before you begin."

Jay looked at Bass, still suffused with fury
and saw himself hung without benefit of jury.
Bass selected the punching bag gloves, the cruelest kind,
to mete out the punishment that he had in mind.
Jay weighed 160 pounds, and was fit as a fiddle
Bass was 250, and fat in the middle.

Bass's punches came in bunches from all conceivable angles
while strutting his stuff like another Bojangles.
Battered and bleeding, Jay refused to go down
though reeling about like a drunken clown.
All this exertion was taking its toll,
Bass was breathing heavily, like a mare in foal.

"Hit'em, Blue Eyes, hit'em," his friends did implore
though to hit a teacher was an irrefutable law.

> To survive, Jay let go with a ponderous right to the jaw
> down and out went Bad Ass; full length on the floor.
> Blue Eyes and Big Nose took off the gloves and quietly
> walked away and became a Brooklyn legend, ever since
> that day.

There is a common axiom among marital therapists—the features you fall in love with in your partner inevitably come to annoy and frustrate you. Gentle stoicism becomes intractable withholding, emotionality becomes mood swings, and the fiery creativity? Attention deficit disorder. Conversely, when it comes to things about your parents, their history, and your own childhood, they thicken over time into a more interesting stew. Did "Blue Eyes and Big Nose" really whip "Mr. Bad Ass?" There's no way I'd ever know, and it didn't really matter. And given my father's love of boxing, it didn't surprise me to read of "punches in bunches" and "a ponderous right to the jaw," phrases my coach John might have used. Still, I was suffused with a fresh wave of the synchronicity shivers. Had my journey been guided all along by a force greater than me?

Here's what I did know: whatever the obstacles, my father and I had both wanted to be strong, or at least to be thought of like that. The Poet Laureate of Plainview may not have taught me to swim, and even contributed mightily to my fears about the world, but he never abandoned the search for the motel with a pool.

The immigrant Jewish boxers struggled with the dilemma that faces all oppressed groups. Am I *too much* of this thing that makes me who I am? Or am I *not enough* of it? It's a no-win situation, and no one is alone in it. Artist Charles Miller, whose portraits of Jewish boxers (Benny Leonard, Barney Ross, countless others) are highly prized, describes them as "anti-heroes, searching for something and as in much of Jewish history, there is a sense of rootlessness in their stories" with whom he feels a profound connection. He painted these boxers, he says, to "put blood back in their bodies again."

Alan Dershowitz spoke of a 'candle theory' of Judaism, suggesting that "the great successes in Judaism are people who moved away from (its) flame," which is of course a controversial idea (he was likely talking about the past helpful function of assimilation), but he is right that the simple fact is "the further you move away from the flame, the less likely you are to have Jewish children and grandchildren." As someone devout, he has concerns about the diminishing of the tribe. "It's a great paradox," he says. "There's no answer. You need to be the right distance away."

The right distance away. John had shown me the importance of establishing my own range in boxing, my own reach. Initially it was mystifying. Did it have to do with the length of my arms? Where I stood in relation to my opponent? When I experienced it physically one day, a world opened up. My proper range was not so far away that I couldn't make contact, but not so close up that I would get lost and smothered. As with boxing, my range from my parents, my father especially, had been just a little too far away, but it couldn't be so close that I would be swallowed up.

I had to find a way to make the connection. That method would be unique to me, and I could only find it by trying. When my range was right, I was "the right distance away," and I had the most power; anything that could emanate from my body, imperfect as it was, would come from that place.

Daniel Mendoza told me that a boxer needs to be in a state of equilibrium, and that state will depend on the unique characteristics of the boxer. Short-armed is different from having a long reach. John told me I'll never be a real "puncher" because I'm not tall and can't do long powerful hits, but I can try to get in close, stay close, and keep boxing, inside.

Each person has to find his or her own range concerning the things that matter, whether it is family, work, beliefs, or relationships, and each individual's method will be unique. Each individual can only find that range by trying. You have to test a few things out.

So when people hear I'm boxing and say, with a mixture of curiosity and concern, "Oooh, how can you *do* that?" I wonder, how can they ask that?

Compared to the grotesque excesses of the larger world, boxing is an elegant containment of aggression, a stage for dramas both universal and exquisitely personal, and I've come to love its clarity.

Most surprisingly, it got me out of my head and into my body, and there, in my body, I got smarter, and I met my family again.

acknowledgments

Anthony Riccio told me writing a book was like looking for god, getting married, and having a baby, all at the same time. It also takes the support and encouragement of many people. Thanks to Martha Kaplan and Bonnie Solow, for suggestions on early stages of the manuscript. All the people I met in the boxing world who generously shared their experiences with me—particularly John Spehar and Jennifer Shettleworth (co-owners of Fighting Fitness Gym in Orange, Connecticut), Sue D'Onofrio, Samantha Dane, Sheila Fox, Joan Sawicki, Ryan White, John Gesmonde, Terry Tumminia-Edwards, Larry Pelletier, Kenny the "Hamden Hammer" Schmidt, Steve Acunto. To my coach, John Spehar, more thanks than I can express here for your exceptional patience, openness, knowledge, and insight, and for providing me with access to many of the experiences documented in this book.

My sisters Susan Bordo and Marilyn Silverman have always been tireless champions of my endeavors (even those that cause them to raise their eyebrows and say "*Hmmm . . .*") They are fantastic women, and together we house the archives of our past.

The Connecticut Woman's Club, who provided me with a scholarship to the Wesleyan Writers Conference, gave me a nudge towards reentering a world of creative writing that I had left behind while pursuing other professional goals.

Thanks to the Beinecke Rare Book and Manuscript Library for an afternoon with Daniel Mendoza.

Ray Terlaga and Charmaine Rhode have become my extended family, along with Elena Dixon, who has been a creative and firm cheerleader. Thank you to Kristin Hale, for making rye bread and, along with her dogs Lucy and Elvy, is a permanent member of my pack. Thank you to Carrie Schaffer for friendship and sartorial consultation.

Thank you to the Shapleigh clan for their love and acceptance.

Many authors along the way, for books about boxing that informed my journey immeasurably—Kasia Boddy's *Boxing: A Cultural History*, Alan Bodner's *When Boxing Was a Jewish Sport*, Douglas Century's *Barney Ross*, Joyce Carol Oates's *On Boxing*, Laila Ali's *Reach Out*, Sander Gilman's *Jewish Frontiers*, Jack Kugelman's *Jews, Sports, and the Rites of Citizenship*, Norman Mailer's *The Fight*, to name just a few.

To Anthony Riccio, who led me to the great people at SUNY Press.

To James Peltz, for helping me make the dream of a book become a reality. To Laurie Searl and Fran Keneston, for helping me deliver this baby.

To Alan Kahn, author of *The Speed Bag Bible*, for providing me with the amazing vintage photo of Belle/Bessie Gordon for the cover, and for exemplifying the responsiveness and generosity of the boxing community.

To artist Charles Miller for images of his remarkable paintings of Jewish boxers for the book trailer.

Special thanks to designer Bill Brown for creating a beautiful and evocative cover.

To Monica Talmor, for her generous help with genealogical research.

To "shtetl-finder," for providing their service to seekers like myself.

Jacob Hunter helped me put on my first pair of boxing gloves and later suggested I find a coach.

Burton Austen, MD, for guidance and wonderful insight along the way, and for his understanding of the value of competition and sports. Ron Bessel, chiropractor, and practitioner of Krav Maga, an intense form of Israeli combat, who tried to help decipher the mystery of my painful leg.

To Hank Paper and all the folks at Best Video in Hamden, Connecticut, for keeping me supplied with boxing films.

Scott Shapleigh has been the best reader and editor, full of brilliance, insight, and humor. He is my "Mountain," and he's always been in my corner.

Boxing publicity photographs from
Sweeney's Boxing and Fitness, Delmar, NY.
Used by permission.